Pandit
Ajoy Chakrabarty

Pandit
Ajoy Chakrabarty
seeker of the music within

SHYAM BANERJI

With a Foreword by
GULZAR

NIYOGI
BOOKS

Published by
NIYOGI BOOKS
Block D, Building No. 77,
Okhla Industrial Area, Phase-I,
New Delhi-110 020, INDIA
Tel: 91-11-26816301, 26818960
Email: niyogibooks@gmail.com
Website: www.niyogibooksindia.com

Text © Shyam Banerji
Cover photograph: Inni Singh
Photographs courtesy: Pandit Ajoy Chakrabarty, unless otherwise indicated.

Editor: K.E. Priyamvada
Design: Shraboni Roy/Shashi Bhushan Prasad

ISBN: 978-93-89136-23-4
Publication: 2019

Printed at: Niyogi Offset Pvt. Ltd., New Delhi, India

contents

Foreword   06

Preface   09

EARTH   13

FIRE   47

WATER   85

AIR   119

SPACE   161

Index   227

foreword

'Ajoy-da'

I know Ajoy-da, but I know him much more after reading his biography now. I always admired him for his singing and extreme humbleness. I admire him a thousandfold more now. He has emerged from such a tough life. A tree grown through hard rocky soil. He is a tall man, much taller than his physical height.

I don't know why he asked me to write the foreword of his biography. I am humbled.

I have learnt much more about life after reading his life story, which I would have missed.

Coming through extreme poverty, as he grew up, listening to the sounds of a loom, which his father *Ajit Chakrabarty* operated at home. He says:

> While he was matching the beat of the loom, it was like seeing colours being woven with musical notes. He taught me to play with *laya*. He made me practise the *laya*, with the beat of the loom—*swara* by *swara*. It was a magical experience I received from my father, my first Guru.

Doesn't he sound like a poet, my Ajoy-da? While reading those passages I could hear the

*Gulzar and Ajoy Chakrabarty
exchanging musical ideas*

click-clack of the loom. That reminded me of an Urdu poem.

मुझको भी तरक़ीब सिखा दे यार जुलाहे!

Teach me a few tricks, Oh dear Weaver,
How do you knit the threads of relationships?

I have heard him singing Tagore. His face takes the expressions of the poet. He sings Qazi Nazrul Islam with the same passion. He has quoted Beethoven so well, saying, 'To play a wrong note is insignificant, but to play without passion is inexcusable'.

This passion Ajoy-da carries in every aspect of life. His attachment with friends and family is exemplary. His passion for fish is similar. He has well narrated the incident of his childhood when he bought the big fish, 'rohu' for the family.

Ajoy-da, knows fish by names and their nature, like you know your pets. I was lucky to have had an opportunity once to relish his chosen fish. That was in Abu Dhabi. He quoted Shakespeare at one juncture with humour, 'If fish be the food of love, "Eat on, eat on!"'

About music he has only one conviction to express, 'I do not know, how right or wrong it is, but I relate to the entire world, *both inside and outside*, only through one thing … that is Music.'

सातों बार बोले बँसी
एक ही बार बोले ना
तन की लागी सारी बोले
मन की लागी बोले ना!

The flute speaks out in seven notes,
There is one note that speaks in silence;
The worldly loves are for all to hear,
The inner soul has to be heard in its quietude.

—GULZAR

preface

Ajoy Chakrabarty and Shyam Banerji   *Photo courtesy: Inni Singh*

The song of life is a duet rendered in two voices—the voice of destiny and the voice of human effort; both the voices are equally important. Singing this song is not about both voices being in harmony, it is more about both voices singing in sync and the human voice rising to respond to the complex musical notes of destiny's challenges and opportunities.

Ancient Sanskrit texts have a beautiful definition of the *swara* or the musical note: *Swayam rãjate iti swarah* (that which revels by itself or that which is resplendent in itself, is *swara*). Every musical note is blessed by the gods to shine on its own. Every time our breath cradles it with devotion, we are one with God.

The music of destiny becomes divine for someone who embraces every *swara* that destiny has placed on the score-sheet of life with gratitude, regardless of the complexities of the *bandish* or the composition of joys and sorrows. Those who are able to shine in their divinely ordained music can say, 'I am my music. My music is His song!' This is the story of such a person.

This book is a journey on the ever flowing Ganges of *Anahad Nada*—the eternal sound, the primordial *swara* or note, that is the fountainhead of all that is within and without … all that we hear and see.

Rowing the boat of memories, emotions and beliefs with Pandit Ajoy Chakrabarty has been a soulfully melodious experience. The river was lined by great sights and sounds. As I rowed, and wrote about what I saw, Pandit Ajoy Chakrabarty broke into many a song. From time to time he dived deep into himself to embellish my narrative with the rhythm of his reminiscences and the raga of his soul. The journey continues. The journey of a yogi never ends!

—SHYAM BANERJI

The River Ganga at Shyamnagar

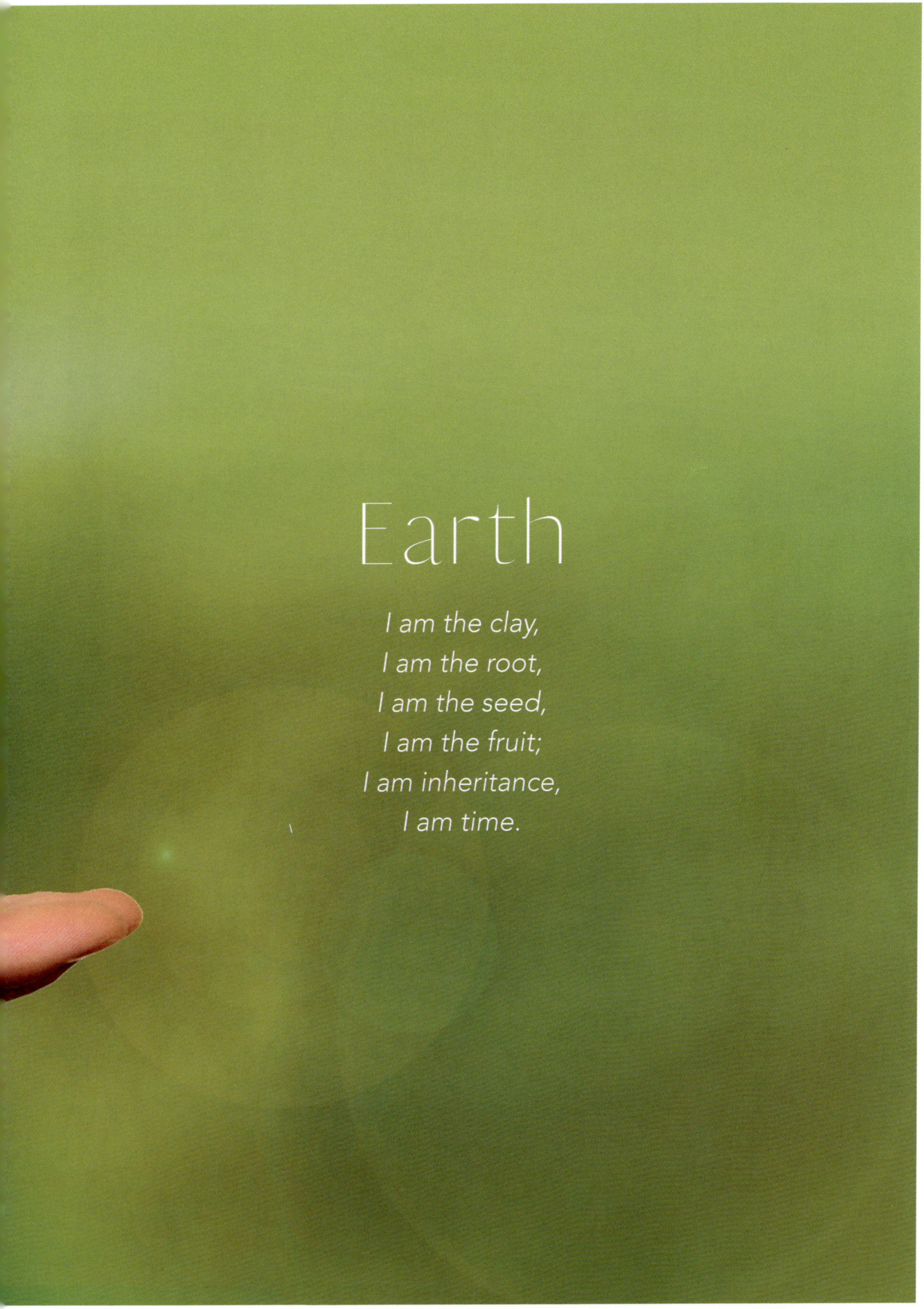

Earth

I am the clay,
I am the root,
I am the seed,
I am the fruit;
I am inheritance,
I am time.

sa

Life begins much before one is born, sometimes generations earlier. Ajoy Chakrabarty's grandfather, a doctor and a wealthy landowner living in Mymensingh (now in Bangladesh) was sure that his son Ajit would also grow up to be a doctor. He was shocked when, one day, Ajit told him that he had no intention of studying medicine. His anger was fanned further when he learnt that Ajit wanted to become a singer. He was sure that Ajit had been influenced by his music-loving *chhoto kaka* (paternal uncle). No way. Ajit's father did not want his son to be associated with 'the immoral, undisciplined world of music and musicians'. But Ajit did not want to have it any other way. Music was Ajit's passion. He wanted to sing. He could think of nothing else. Ajit's passion for music called for a parting of ways with his father and in 1933, 19-year-old Ajit found himself on the unfamiliar streets of Kolkata, which was then a city in the throes of turmoil and change.

Kolkata had ceased to be the capital of British India in 1911. Wounds were raw. The scars of the division of Bengal by the British were still painful. Dissent wafted in the air. The spirit of nationalism

Facing page, top and above: Young Ajoy Chakrabarty

Ajoy Chakrabarty with his father, two mothers, brother and family

echoed in the streets. The memory of revolutionaries Badal-Benoy-Dinesh's assassination of the British Inspector General of Prisons in Kolkata's busy Writers' Building in 1930 was still fresh. The firebrand freedom fighter Surya Sen had been arrested early in 1933. Subhash Chandra Bose had upped his ante against British imperialism as well as the pacifists in the Indian National Congress. There was strife. There was struggle. There was anger. There was hope. It was not easy to find work. Ajit Chakrabarty had no money and had to spend many a night without a morsel of food. But he was not one to go back. His self-respect and his faith in God did not permit it. Throughout his life, these two were to be his greatest assets and his greatest treasures.

Ajit's first home in Kolkata was a makeshift bamboo and tarpaulin shanty on the pavement near the famed Kali temple of Kalighat. Many believe that the name Kolkata is derived from the word Kalighat. Here, in the protective shade of Goddess Kali, Ajit found another melodious nearness. Ajit's shanty was below the house of two music stalwarts. Their *riyaaz* and music lessons spilled over to the pavement. Ajit had chosen the spot well. He soaked himself in the new *swara*s in his life but, unfortunately,

Ajoy Chakrabarty with a picture of Ustad Bade Ghulam Ali Khan, his inspiration

like the less-privileged tribal prince Ekalavya, who in the *Mahabharata* learnt archery by hiding and watching Guru Dronacharya teach Prince Arjuna and his brothers. Years flew like arrows from the quiver of time. Those were years of struggle. Unknown to him, this struggle was to become an ocean of self-belief on which he would one-day set sail the musical brilliance of his yet-to-be-born son.

Ajit was 25 when his father, who had by now more or less reconciled to his son's independent thinking, arranged Ajit's marriage with Mahamaya Devi. The *Devimahatmya* (the magnanimity of the goddess), an ancient Indian scripture, refers to Goddess Mahamaya as a form of *Shakti* that metamorphosed from the energy of all the gods. Mahamaya Devi was destined to epitomise this reference. Destiny, however, had written a song for Mahamaya Devi in which one part was to remain unsung. This part had also been foretold by her family's spiritual guide Premananda Tirthaswami Maharaj. Mahamaya Devi was not destined to bear children.

After 11 years of childlessness and after the doctors confirmed that Mahamaya Devi would not be able to bear children, Mahamaya and Ajit's parents proposed

Ajoy Chakrabarty's family guru, Sreemat Premananda Tirthaswamiji Maharaj

Ajit's marriage to Mahamaya Devi's younger sister, Jayanti Devi. With Mahamaya Devi's concurrence, Ajit Chakrabarty's second marriage also took place.

On 25 December 1952, as the world celebrated Christmas, a son was born to Jayanti Devi and this unique *tridhara* (triple stream) of marital love and happiness. Premananda Tirthaswami Maharaj had predicted the birth of Ajit's son years ago. Years ago he had also given the name... *Ajoy.* Ajoy Chakrabarty.

As a child I simply knew that I have two mothers and that I belong to both. Unlike other children, when I learnt to speak, I began with two sets of words—*Bado Ma* and *Chhoto Ma* (Elder Mother and Younger Mother). I

grew up calling the woman who gave birth to me as my '*Chhoto Ma'*—my younger mother.

My elder mother was like a Maharishi. A sage! The Mother Goddess! When I look back, I do not remember any of my friends calling my elder mother Mahamaya Devi anything other than Ma... 'Mother'. She was Sarvanandamayi Ma... the mother who bestows joy on all. She became the substratum of my life like the Divine Mother in her incarnation as Jagatdhatri—the beholder of the world. My world!

Some may find these circumstances amusing. Well, it is out of the ordinary for sure. It is extra-ordinary—an extra-ordinary good fortune of mine—to be loved by two mothers and that too, so much!

re

Mulajore Kali Temple, Shyamnagar

A few years before Ajoy's birth, Ajit Chakrabarty had settled down in Shyamnagar on the banks of the Ganga, about 30 miles upstream from Kolkata. Shyamnagar was then a small town surrounded by extensive wetlands.

Here on a piece of land not far from Shyamnagar's famous Mulajore Kali Temple, Ajit Chakrabarty had made his home—a modest dwelling that had more open spaces than rooms. The rooms had tiled roofs. The tiles added

Ajoy Chakrabarty with his father and two mothers

to the music of the monsoons with more than an occasional leak. Ajoy Chakrabarty was born in this house.

With the passage of time most of Shyamnagar's wetlands have been engulfed by its now huge population. The open spaces of the Chakrabarty home have also now given way to many new rooms—rooms that wait eagerly to listen to the chatter of friends and relatives during the Durga Puja hosted by the family every year.

The courtyard remains almost unchanged—like the stage of a *jatra* (a form of Bengali folk theatre) on which memories enact themselves year after year. The courtyard still has the *Thakur ghar* (deity's room) on one side. It was the hub of all activities—work, leisure and whatever pleasure lack of money could afford.

The little boy prancing in the courtyard under the watchful gaze of his father and the doting eyes of two mothers only came to know in his high school years that the day he was born his parents did not have three *paise* needed for buying 'honey', which, in those days, was ritually touched to a newborn's mouth with prayers to ensure a life honeyed with joy and glory.

Ajit Chakrabarty was a melodious singer. He had a powerful high-pitched voice. He loved singing *kirtan*s and *Shyama sangeet* (songs in praise of Goddess Shyama or Kali). Artistes like Krishna Chandra Dey, Kundan Lal Saigal and Mrinal Kanti Ghosh were some of the most famous singers during Ajit Chakrabarty's young days and he rendered their songs brilliantly.

With the lighting of the *sandhya* (the evening lamp) and the call of the conch, the darkness of wants and needs in the Chakrabarty house were dispelled for some time by the impassioned singing of kirtans and bhajans (genres of devotional songs). Neighbours trooped to the courtyard to join the chorus of hope and faith in the bounties of Hari and Kali. When they joined the Chakrabarty family in singing '*Aami maayer haathe*

khai pori, Maa niyechhen aamar bhaar' (I am fed and clothed by the mother, the mother has me in her care), it was first a statement of faith and then a song. It was the truth of a life of relentless struggle between self-sacrifices and self-esteem.

Little Ajoy was a keen listener and learner and needed very little cajoling and encouragement to sing. These soirees taught Ajoy his earliest and most important lessons as a singer. The lesson that truth makes the most melodious sound and that a song sung without belief is like a sailless boat that does not travel far.

When Ajit heard Ajoy sing for the first time he realised that the voice of divinity was singing through his son. He remembered that Premananda Tirthaswami Maharaj had prophesied that his son would one day become a very well-known singer. Ajit Chakrabarty had given up a world of luxuries to pursue his passion for music. He could not make it big. Extreme poverty had taken a toll on his health too. Now he saw a mirror of fulfilment in his son. He saw an opportunity to transcreate the grace of god that we refer to as 'talent' or 'potential' into a way of life. He saw an opportunity to transform his dream into his son's reality. Standing on the banks of the Ganga, Ajit decided that he would cross the deepest waters to ensure that his son Ajoy sailed very far.

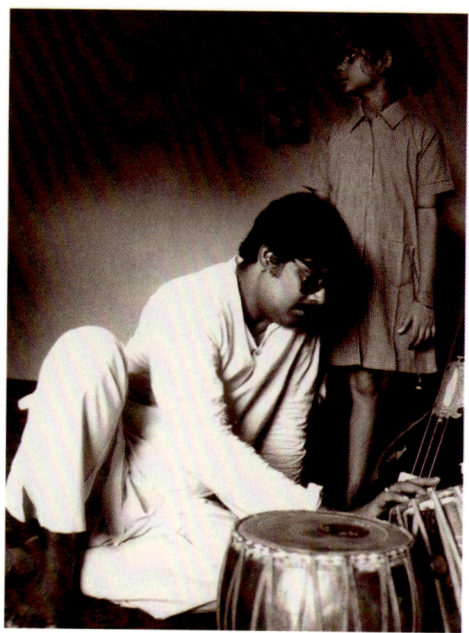

Young Ajoy Chakrabarty

decided to turn herself to face the river, which was to her west, so that she could see and hear her impassioned devotee for as long as she could.

The ferry still crosses over from Mulajore Ferry Ghat to Telinipara on the opposite bank of the Ganga. The crossing was less noisy in the 1950s. Perched on the steamer, Ajoy enjoyed crossing the Ganga with his father's Kali kirtan group when it travelled to render kirtans in Bhadreshwar. There were longer journeys on the Ganga—for performances in Chandan Nagar, Chinsurah and other places. The group's repertoire included the cult-status compositions of legendary Premik Maharaj immortalised by the Andul Kali temple kirtan singers. These were lyrics and music that had swirled Sri Ramakrishna Paramahansa into a trance and sent Swami Vivekananda into rapture.

Ajit knew that Goddess Kali would answer his prayers. The Goddess of the Mulajore Kali temple in Shyamnagar was known for her magnanimity. Unlike most other Kali idols, the idol here faces west and not south—the traditional direction in which Goddess Kali is supposed to face. Legend has it that one of her great devotees, Sadhak Ramprasad, the famed *Shakta* poet of the 18th century, used to sail past the temple singing her glories in his soulful voice. The goddess always implored him to stay awhile and sing to her but, lost in his trance, Ramprasad never broke his journey or his song. So Mother Kali of Mulajore

Dhrupad was the foundation of these kirtans. Challenging rhythm patterns like *Chautal*, *Teevra* and *Dhamaar* teased the rhythm-universe of little Ajoy. There were complex shifts in patterns within compositions. For a three-year-old boy it was a Goddess-sent learning experience. '*Jai Ma Kali! Jai Guru!*' Little Ajoy enjoyed lending his voice to these chants too.

ga

Ajoy Chakrabarty with his gurujis; (left) Guru Sadananda Brahmachary Maharaj and (right) Guru Jnan Prakash Ghosh

Marriage brings new responsibilities. Parenthood brings even more. Ajit Chakrabarty realised that singing kirtans could not be the only livelihood for and his family. The fabric of life needed a new *tana-bana*—a new warp and weft, a new loom. And that is exactly what Ajoy's parents turned to—a hand-weaving loom that Ajit had acquired in a dismantled condition from Mymensingh some years ago. It was time to set it up. Ajit had learnt carpentry too. Perhaps that skill could also be put to remunerative use now.

Sujani is a unique Indian quilt or a wrap made from recycled sarees. It is also the name for the stitch associated with its making. India's folklore has a deep connection with its crafts and rituals. The word sujani is derived from 'su' meaning 'to facilitate' and 'jani' meaning 'birth' or 'life'. In other words, 'to facilitate or nurture life'. Nothing could have been more symbolic for little Ajoy's future or for Ajit Chakrabarty's dream for him.

There is also an age-old tradition associated with the weaving of sujanis, especially in some areas of Bihar and Jharkhand. In these regions, there is a goddess of sujani known as Chitiriya Mata (literally meaning 'Mother Goddess of Tatters'). What could have been more apt for the struggling Chakrabarty household in those days?

> I do not know how right or wrong it is, but I relate to the entire world, both inside and outside me, only through one thing … music. When I look back on the courtyard as it was when I was a child, I hear the soulful strains of a *bandish* being sung in *jugalbandi* (duet) by my mothers. If I put lyrics to it, then it would go something like this…

बिनती करूँ मैं चितरिया माँ,
बुन दे सुजनिया ख़ुशियन की
सुख दुःख का मैं धागा पिरोऊँ,
भाग जगा दे दुःखियन की।

Lift the fortunes of this sorrowful one,
Oh Goddess of Tatters, I pray to thee.
I put together the threads of joy and sorrow,
Create a sujani of happiness for me!

Heaps of old sarees and dhotis took over Ajoy's beloved courtyard. Added to this was the dust that flew around when his mothers cleaned the fabric. Ajoy was amused by the way some of the old sarees were cut into strips, twined around and woven on the loom. He was too young to realise that for his parents he was the most important fabric and that for them his future was the most important weave. The fabric of Ajoy's childhood was created by the sacrifices woven by his parents.

A sujani sold for only three rupees. The occasional kantha saree fetched a little more—five rupees! It was hard labour. When he grew up and could make the walk to the neighbouring settlements on his own, Ajoy helped his parents in delivering the sujanis to the doorstep of those who had placed orders. Many times, after having delivered the sarees, Ajoy was asked to come again to collect the payment at a more convenient time. Sometimes he had to make many trips to collect the very modest returns for his parents' toils.

The loom wove many lessons for Ajoy. He would always remember that there is no alternative to hard work and that the biggest joy of working comes from working for the joy of others. The loom also gave Ajoy his first guru—someone who remained the most uncompromising, unrelenting and yet most lovable guru of his life—his father Ajit Chakrabarty.

Young Ajoy Chakrabarty accompanying his Guru Jnan Prakash Ghosh

The click-clack of the loom was a rhythm that I soon got used to. What I loved most was my father calling me and asking me to sit on his lap while he wove the cloth. Matching the beat of the loom, he made me practise the *sargam*. I followed him *swara* by *swara*. At times, he made the mathematics of the movement from one *swara* to the other a bit more difficult. He taught me to play with *laya*. He taught me that *laya* or tempo is life. He taught me that this *laya* is sacrosanct and that we have to beautify it with the right *swaras* at the right time with the right intensity. He also taught me to give up all thoughts of trying to escape from his lap till I got the notes right. Not even if Bado Ma or Chhoto Ma called me for food! Actually, I also never felt like getting off. It was a magical experience. It was like seeing a collage of colours being woven together with musical notes. I could feel and see music 'happening' in the fabric right there in front of me. I did not have the understanding to put the experience in such words then, but I found it absolutely enchanting. My father, my first guru, gave my music a 'soul'. He gave me the essence of my being what I am, and the essentiality of the habit of seeing music everywhere and revelling in music at all times.

A perfect weave demands coordination between mind and body. The weaver has to attain harmony of thought, motion and rhythm to create a unique product. A raga in the hands of a performer is no different.

Years later the legendary sarangi maestro and guru, Pandit Hanuman Prasad Misraji heard me and said, 'You play with *laya*. May god bless you.' On hearing this, my father smiled and said, 'Well it pays to listen to a heavy dose of *chautal*, *teevra* and *dhamaar* at a very young age.' He was referring to the kirtan sessions.

When I look back on those memories I think I have followed the main lesson of the loom that excellence is about being in rhythm and yet not being enslaved by it. And it is also about making sacrifices…

ma

Ajoy Chakrabarty practising music with his father, Ajit Chakrabarty

When people refuse to stop dreaming in the face of acute poverty, something has to bear the brunt of the struggle. Two decades of a self-respecting fight against all odds had taken a toll on Ajit Chakrabarty's health, especially his lungs. Music continued, but a major part of Ajit Chakrabarty's time was now spent at the Ichhapur Northland High School, where he had gained employment as a teacher in the primary section. Surrounded by children, he realised that a talented child is like a gushing river, whose course needs to be well directed and whose banks need to be really strong. If the talent was prodigious, as was the case of his son Ajoy, then there was no time to waste. The river had to be put on track!

By the age of four Ajoy had learnt many songs from his father. He had struck up a great friendship with the seven notes. The hoots of the streamers plying on the Ganga, the chirping of birds that flitted around in the courtyard, the whistling of the train, the call of the cows in their cowshed … there were many kinds of music around him. Little did he know then that a new love-soaked musical note was about to enter the raga of his life—the sound of the bell of Guru Pannalal Babu's cycle.

When he was a little over four-years-old, Ajoy's father told him, 'Paanu sings very well. I think he will be a good teacher for you,' and so little Ajoy found his first formal guru—Shri Pannalal Samanta, who was also Ajit Chakrabarty's friend.

Shri Pannalal Samanta was the epitome of goodness. He worked in the Ichhapore Rifle Factory and like most people at that time in Shyamnagar he rode a cycle. Ajoy looked forward to his arrival, not just for his music lessons but also for the *chiniwala* (sugary) biscuit that he brought for Ajoy. The lozenges that Pannalal Babu brought and the opportunity to do a 'half-pedal' on his cycle were other things Ajoy looked forward to. The 'half-pedal'—a way of riding a cycle when one is not tall enough to reach the pedals from the seat—was great fun. Classes of course were more serious and more focused, but Pannalal Babu made them enjoyable too.

The idea behind getting Pannalal Babu as Ajoy's guru was to groom him into a system of disciplined training. Pannalal Babu's mode of teaching

Ajoy Chakrabarty

was an extension of parental love. The curriculum was rudimentary—*sargams*, some bhajans and a few classical compositions—but it is these early years that cement a student's love for music, or any other art or any subject that has the potential to be the sub-stratum of the student's future. Pannalal Babu did that beautifully. Brick by brick he helped in building the edifice of Ajoy's basic understanding of the *swara* and *swara*-patterns with the mortar of abounding love and honesty.

When my curious mind asked Pannalal Babu a question to which he did not have a direct answer, he had the magnanimity to say, 'Babu Ajoy, I don't know. But we will find out…' He gave me my first tabla lessons too. He was a very fine tabla player. Classes did not end with the dictum, 'You must become a good singer'. That was understood. That was ingrained. Classes ended with the advice, 'Be a good person. Good people sing more beautifully'.

When Ajoy was six, his father admitted him in Ichhapur Northland High School—the same school where he was employed as a teacher. Ajit was clear that academics and formal education were not to be compromised in the pursuit of music. As per his age, Ajoy was given direct admission to the third standard by the school's principal Shri Brojendra Kumar Dey.

Ichhapur Northland High School was a little more than three km from his home. In the initial years, Ajoy went with his father on a cycle and in later years by local bus and train. School was fun. It also brought out Ajoy's other talents.

I remember my headmaster Shri Brojendra Kumar Dey lifting me on his shoulder with great joy after my performance as Sri Krishna in the musical play *Rajsanyasi*. I sang four songs in it. My father who had composed the songs was not in favour of my playing the part because he did not want me to get any preference as the composer's son but Brojendra Babu insisted and I got to play the role. I also remember doing the lead in Bangla plays like *Kala Pahad* and *Karan-Arjun*.

There was some learning that got imprinted forever, like my winning the second prize on two occasions for reciting Sukumar Ray's popular nonsense-verse '*Ei daekho pencil, note boi e haathe*' in two different recitation competitions. Loosely translated it means, 'Look at this pencil and the notebook in this hand'. On the first occasion the judge, legendary theatre personality Shri Ahindra Choudhury told my father, 'I would have surely given him the first prize if he had taken a pencil in his hand and used it for some actions.'

Young Ajoy Chakrabarty begins his journey into the world of music

In the next competition where the great Shri Sishir Bhaduri was the judge, I took up a pencil very diligently and spoke my heart out. I came second again. Sishir Babu told my father, 'Your son spoke the best. But why did you have to have a pencil in his hand?'

The prizes remained my childhood's pride. From time to time they were dusted clean. The lesson stayed vibrantly clear. My father drove it into me over the years that viewpoints can differ but the right to have a different view has to be respected even if one does not agree with it. I remember him always telling me, even when I had grown up, 'You do your part as best as you can. Never feel judged and try not to judge others.' It is a difficult path to follow but I have tried to follow it. But then there are emotions and sometimes they do come in the way. When they do, I try to rise to his advice even more.

It all seems like yesterday. I am glad that I have been able to build some good memories. Good memories help us to accept the not-so-good ones with humility and gratitude. I do not have many photos of my childhood. Photos were a luxury. But I cherish two photos—I am talking of photos in which only I feature. In the first one, I can be seen posing with my trophies. Most of them have nothing to do with music. It reminds me that I put aside many desires to focus on learning music. In the other photo I am posing with my tanpura. I am sitting on the floor. Behind me is a fence of bamboo shafts and leaves. The fence encapsulates the difficult environment in which I had to learn music in my childhood. It also sums up my parents' tenacity to ensure that regardless of all obstacles, I kept learning music.

The fence that can be seen in the picture had a cowshed on one side. Here little Ajoy had a devoted fan, Lakshmi, one of the cows. Every time Ajoy practised, she would make her way towards him and listen to him singing. Music connects with everything in so many, still-unexplained, ways. Ajoy was inspired to go deep into these connections one day.

pa

Ajoy was growing. Not only had he grown taller, his world had grown larger too in terms of exposure to new emotions and experiences. He had started revelling in his love for music. He had also started understanding that his family was financially tight. His parents had brought him up with such dignity and self-respect that he did not immediately connect this to the hard fact that his family was actually far from being financially well-off. He was too young to understand the dynamics of being poor or to understand why his father always bought smaller fish from the fish market while others bought larger ones—the *rohu*s and *hilsa*s. He was tired of eating the much smaller fishes—*khoira, morola, kholshe* and *puti*.

So, one day he took some money from the pocket of his father's kurta, which was hanging on the *aalna* (a traditional clothes hanger). With his pocketful of stolen money Ajoy went to the fish market and bought a huge *rohu* (freshwater carp) that cost Rs 32. That day, he walked home with pride. Everyone was looking at him and his fish. Meanwhile, his father was looking for his son and his missing 50 rupees.

Ajoy reached home to a stunned reception. *Bado Ma* and *Chhoto Ma* were stunned by the size of the fish. Ajit Chakrabarty was stunned by what his son had done. Ajoy had nowhere to hide. The fish was too big to hide anyway. Ajit Chakrabarty understood why Ajoy had done what he had. He looked deep into Ajoy's eyes. As Ajoy lowered his gaze, he heard a soft voice that echoed louder than anything he had heard before, 'Don't do it again, son! Never fall prey to temptation'. Ajoy looked up. A lot was said silently by both, as their eyes met.

My father read my mind and my emotions. I promised never to do it again. He never disbelieved me because I never lied. I also scored some points for my truthfulness. But I had created a huge problem. In a household that lived on small fish, there was no knife that could cut such a big fish! And so I had to take it back to the Dunbar Mill fish market to get it cut. Refrigerators were a novelty in the late 1950s and the nearest refrigerator must have been miles away. I don't remember having seen one at that age anyway. So, the fish had to be consumed the same day. I had a feast that night. Fortunately or unfortunately

A good teacher, however, always stays with a good disciple.

Pandit Ajoy Chakrabarty shares his fondness for fish

the neighbourhood too had a feast because the rest of the fish had to be distributed.

Ajoy learnt from Pannalal Babu for two very important years. Pannalal Babu unleashed the flow of Ajoy's innate musical nature. He pushed the stream over the waterfall's edge. When the waterfall gathered momentum and Pannalal Babu felt it would not be right for him to hold Ajoy back, he waited a bit longer after the class to meet Ajoy's father. The tea that *Chhoto Ma* offered him as he waited tasted both happy and sad. It had the taste of parting—the sweet bitterness of letting someone move on for the better.

When my father came in, Pannalal Babu said, 'Well, I have taught Ajoy what I could. I think he should now learn from my guru, Shri Kanaidas Bairagi. He is a very fine disciple of the legendary Guru Jnan Prakash Ghosh Babu. He will make a perfect teacher for our Ajoy.'

My mothers had gathered around us by now.

'Where does Kanaidas Babu stay?' my Bado Ma asked.

'Naihati,' said Guru Pannalalji.

'Naihati? But that is so far from here for a 6-year-old. How will he go? He has his school too,' Chhoto Ma said.

'Yes, Didi! And the school is in the opposite direction!' Pannalal Babu smiled that soothing, love-filled smile of his.

He put his hand on my head, looked at my mothers and said, 'This is just the beginning. He has to go very far. He has to make many journeys. Prepare him for it. Prepare yourselves for it.'

And so began the journey of my gurus becoming my guru-bhais. How does one define a 'guru-bhai?'... I guess male disciples of the same guru!

LEFT AND BELOW:
*Mulajore Kali Temple,
Shyamnagar*

The railway station at Shyamnagar

The inaugural plaque at the new booking office of Shyamnagar railway station bears the name of Pandit Ajoy Chakrabarty

dha

Ajoy Chakrabarty's father teaching music to young children

Naihati is about 8 km from Shyamnagar, upstream along the river Ganga. Even in the late 1950s there was a regular bus and train service between the two towns, but one had to wait much longer than one has to today. For the next 10 years, this route became Ajoy's highway to self-exploration and search for excellence.

Whoever said 'seeing is believing' could not have been more incorrect—to believe is to see! Ajoy was entering a world in which he was about to learn a lot more about the art of seeing the unseen, along with the art of looking within. A world in which both 'the heard' as well as 'the unheard' sounds were supreme! Guru Kanaidas Bairagi could not see—'see' in the physical sense of the word. He was sight-less. Ajoy had never envisioned that he would need to spend so much time with someone

Guru Kanaidas Bairagi
Source: You Tube

Guru Kanaidas Bairagi put a calming hand on my head and blessed me lovingly. He said that Pannalal Babu had talked very highly of me. He was so full of love. Almost as sweet as Guru Pannalal Samanta's chiniwala biscuits! I felt comfortable in my new classroom. I also knew that I had to come only once a week. I did not know then that I would soon want to come again and again.

But there was a problem ... to learn from Guru Kanaidas Bairagi, I needed to have my own tanpura. The cost of a good tanpura was Rs 90. It was almost the same as my father's salary. The maths was all wrong; the equation was not right. However, my father was a man on a mission— 'Mission Ajoy.' There were no two thoughts in his mind. Compromising with anything to do with my music was out of the question. The tanpura had to be bought. He took a loan from a money lender, a 'kabuliwalah' at an interest of Rs 8 per month. In giving me my tanpura, my father, and with him my two mothers, gave me a part of their lives. In the months that followed, as my interest in music took deeper roots, the debt and the kabuliwalah's interest flowered too. In the end my father ended up paying Rs 300.

My first harmonium had cost Rs 36. The kabuliwalah had a role to play in making that happen too. Of course,

devoid of sight and that too at such a young age.

No one had told me that Guru Kanaidas Bairagi could not see. So, it was a surprise that sent many thoughts running in my mind when I first saw him. He wore dark glasses. Like most other people I was also used to reading expressions and reactions in the eyes of the people with whom I interacted. This was a different world.

In a way, it was good that I had not been briefed about his handicap. I had gone there thinking about how I would learn, what I would do, how I would sing. On seeing my new music teacher, my thoughts went out to him. He must have read my thoughts.

I don't remember whether it was the same kabuliwalah, though it could have been. All I remembered as I grew up was that I had so much to be thankful to my parents for. No, I am not talking of money. That is unimportant in comparison to what they really gave me—love. Money can be paid back but how does one repay love? Like the *swara* it echoes on its own and the echo never ends.

Ajoy's Naihati years were destined to be an amazing period not just for the development of his music and but also his persona. To begin with, accepting his guru's sightlessness was a bit of a challenge for a boy of six but the presence of other students and that of his *Chhoto Ma* helped him ease into his new environment—an environment in which 'sound' was king, queen, courtier and god. Sound became the cornerstone of Ajoy's relationship with his guru.

As the years went by, Ajoy understood that his sightless guru was able to see him and his tremendous potential better than most others. The word 'blind' disappeared from Ajoy's vocabulary for all time to come. The word *swara* itself took on a whole new world of meaning that left behind textbook limitations of its definition. Seeing the *swara* was about seeing with the mind's eye.

Ajoy Chakrabarty

Many students learnt from Guru Kanaidas Bairagi but he delighted in teaching Ajoy and eagerly waited for him. The classes had no time limit; they could go on for hours. Ajoy reached Guru Kanaidas Bairagi's modest home on the banks of the Ganga in the morning. *Chhoto Ma* generally accompanied him on the train journey from Shyamnagar to Naihati.

I learnt for about 10 years from Guru Kanaidas Bairagi. I used to call him Master Moshai. Every Sunday, and sometimes on weekdays too, I reached his house early in the morning. Even as I was taking off my slippers outside his room, Master Moshai would ask, 'Ajoy?

You have arrived? Good. Come in.' Just from the sound of my slippers he knew that it was me. It was not that I was the only student. There were others too but his amazing ability to distinguish the nature and content of sound intrigued the child in me. This child in me lives on. Maybe that is why teaching music to children gives me so much joy. Sometimes I waited outside with my mother as Guruji finished teaching others. Even then, his teaching rang in my ears. It created a wondrous collage in my mind as I watched what my Guru could not see—the everyday humdrum of life passing by on the road and on the river.

Sometimes when I got on the train to Naihati, I could not help but think about the difficult times that Master Moshai must have gone through. I am not talking of his loss of eyesight. I had come to know that Master Moshai's father had been a wandering singer on the local train network and that he had brought up his son with the alms that he received from music-loving passengers. My guru had inherited his mellifluous voice from him. This left a deep imprint on my mind. After that, every time I got off the train and made my way to his house, I surrendered at his feet with a deeper sense of humility and admiration. To this day, every time I see a child singing for a living on the roadside or on a train it sends me into a spiral of emotions.

At any point of time there were six to eight students in Guru Kanaidas Bairagi's class. Some were older than Ajoy. The student who paid 50 paise for the month was as welcome at Guru Kanaidas Bairagi's altar of learning as the one who paid Rs seven or eight. He never expected or desired more. This divinely selfless approach to teaching reflected in Guru Kanaidas Bairagi's soulful voice. This divinity glowed through the dark glasses that covered his sightless eyes. Ajoy found a new dawn in them.

Learning from Guru Kanaidas Bairagi was as thrilling as swimming through a wondrous, maze-like network of streams. Ajoy loved losing himself in this maze. One day found Ajoy floating away on a bhajan and the next few days found him diving deep into a raga. There were no set rules. Teaching and learning rode the waves of inner instincts. These instincts became the unseen, unspoken language between the two. The 'traditional learning' curriculum with its stepping-stones of a pre-set sequence of ragas was set aside and the doors of a vast palace of music were flung open for Ajoy. From *Bhoopali* little Ajoy moved to *Bhatiyar*. This was not the norm. People who could not see where Guru Kanaidas Bairagi was taking Ajoy, taunted that nothing better could be expected from

Photo courtesy: Inni Singh

Ajoy Chakrabarty

a sightless singer. Ajoy, of course, never realised that he was defying norms. When he grew up to realise that his training had been different, he was glad that his teachers had never been slaves to norms. He remained absolutely at ease with the satisfaction of his having been able to sing Raga *Bhatiyar* before a local audience when he was less than eight years old. In one of these childhood programmes, Ajoy was accompanied on the tabla by a boy called Anindo, who was a couple of years younger than Ajoy. Anindo grew up to become famous the world over as tabla maestro Pandit Anindo Chatterjee.

Yaman, Jaunpuri, Behag… Ajoy's world was full of new melodies, new notes, new experiences. Guru Kanaidas Bairagi was also very fond of singing and teaching Kali kirtans, bhajans and songs of other kinds. This added many colours to Ajoy's love for music from a very young age. Guru Kanaidas Bairagi was also a wizard on the tabla and the harmonium. His brilliance on the two instruments inspired Ajoy to learn to play the tabla and the harmonium seriously. All this helped Ajoy embrace many kinds of music seamlessly.

Since I had been taught some very complex ragas at a young age, and had been kept away from the conditioning that 'this' raga cannot be sung because 'that' raga has not been learnt yet, I never felt burdened by a sense of being unprepared for any attempt to render any raga. I approached new ragas, new genres, new *baani*s without any inhibitions and I found that they were as eager to take me in their embrace as I was ready to embrace them.

Guru Kanaidas Bairagi loved giving attention to Ajoy. Sometimes he came to Ajoy's house, especially during his school exams, so that Ajoy could focus more on his studies.

Ajoy Chakrabarty in contemplative mood

I have very fond memories of learning from Master Moshai. His little house—a room less than 10 square feet with a little verandah—was near the head of the lane that led away from the river front. Lakshmi Babu's sweet shop was within calling distance. Lakshmi Babu's *modak*s (sweet dumplings) were famous in Naihati. Lakshmi Babu was a very good tabla player too.

The short walk from Naihati Station to Guruji's house had a delightful stopover that became a divinely tasty ritual at Sukumar's *kochuri* shop. It was reason enough to visit Naihati. The classes seemed incomplete without four *kochuri*s from Sukumar's shop in my stomach. I think Shakespeare meant something totally different when he wrote, 'If music be the *food* of love, play on. It should be 'eat on!'

Poltu Da accompanied us on tabla during the classes. Naihati gave me my earliest public audience on the street outside Master Moshai's house. Master Moshai's neighbours congregated around the house when I learnt from him. I remain grateful to each one of them. Why? Every week they made me feel like a performer. Week after week, their expectations inspired me to learn something new and work harder.

When I look back, it seems so mystical that one who could not see, gave my music the *drishti* (vision) to see so much more in myself, in my music, in the ever-shining world of the musical notes and in the almighty's ever glowing songs.

ni

Ajoy learnt from Guru Kanaidas Bairagi till the age of 16. Then history repeated itself. Like Pannalal Babu, Guru Kanaidas Bairagi introduced and handed over Ajoy to his own guru, the legendary musicologist, music composer and versatile singer and instrumentalist, Guru Jnan Prakash Ghosh in 1968. Ajoy had not yet completed 16 years.

Shyamnagar to Naihati, Naihati to Kolkata. The journey was getting bigger and the path was getting wider. The pace was picking up too. Ajoy's father,

Ajit Chakrabarty, was very happy on hearing Guru Kanaidas Bairagi's decision to pass the baton to his master. Guru Jnan Prakash Ghosh was an institution by himself. Ajoy Chakrabarty's father said a prayer to Goddess Kali as he always did and to his spiritual Guru Premananda Tirthaswami Maharaj and looked at Ajoy's mothers. He said, 'My friend Paanu had been so right that evening 10 years ago. Remember his words? He had said, "He has to make many journeys. We should be prepared for it."'

Ajoy Chakrabarty seeks the blessings of his Guru Jnan Prakash Ghosh

Even after I started learning from Guru Jnan Prakash Ghosh, I stayed in regular touch with Master Moshai. When he fell ill about 3 years later, he gave me the responsibility of conducting his classes under his supervision. The classes had students who were much elder to me and had been learning from Master Moshai from much earlier.

Today, not much of Guru Kanaidas Bairagi's singing is available to the world. What remains are some rare recordings. There was an endearing soulfulness in his singing. The same was there in his teaching too. Like my bonding with my dear 'sugar coated-biscuit' guru, Shri Pannalal Samanta, my bonding with my Master Moshai, Guru Kanaidas Bairagi, was also a bond of love, emotionally tied with the threads of music.

One of the significant developments in Ajoy's life happened during his tutelage under Guru Kanaidas Bairagi. One can debate if it would or would not have happened in the way it did, if Ajoy had learnt from someone other than Guru Kanaidas Bairagi—because it was he who introduced young Ajoy to the music of the legend with whom Ajoy's singing was destined to get intrinsically connected.

Guru Kanaidas Bairagi was a devoted fan of Ustad Bade Ghulam Ali Khan Saheb,

*Ustad Bade Ghulam
Ali Khan*
Source: wikipedia.com

the doyen of the Kasur-Patiala gharana. Time and again he talked about Ustad Bade Ghulam Ali Khan Saheb in the class. Quite unknowingly, he also gave Ajoy a dream of learning from Ustad Bade Ghulam Ali Khan Saheb himself.

Master Moshai used to get ecstatic while describing Ustad Bade Ghulam Ali Khan's singing. 'Oh, what a fantastic performance Ghulam Ali Khan Saheb gave the other day!' 'There is no one like him. He is so great and yet so humble!' 'Ghulam Ali Khan Saheb plays with *swaras*!' Master Moshai sowed the seeds of my fascination for Ustad Bade Ghulam Ali Khan. With each sentence, he painted a picture of an ideal that I was searching for and so there was an instant connection when I heard a recording of Ustad Bade Ghulam Ali Khan Saheb for the first time. It was a spiritual connection. I had found my hero, my demigod, my altar.

Ajoy hoped that he would meet Ustad Bade Ghulam Ali Khan Saheb if only to just take his blessings. It is said that

Ustad Bade Ghulam Ali khan with (left) Ustad Barkat Ali Khan and (centre) Nishi Babu, a friend

Ajoy Chakrabarty on the lawn of ITC Sangeet Research Academy

desires that are pure and fervently prayed for, come true. One day, sometime in the summer of 1966, Ajoy's desire came true in the corridors of All India Radio, Kolkata. As he was walking he saw Ustad Bade Ghulam Ali Khan coming his way on a wheelchair, accompanied by Ustad Munawar Ali Khan and well-known vocalist Pandit Prasun Banerjee. Ajoy touched his feet and Bade Ghulam Ali Khan Saheb blessed him, saying '*Jeetey raho beta*' (have a long life, son). God and his devotee were face to face. In that one seemingly small gesture the corridor turned into a place of worship. That day God could not have known that the teenaged devotee who was now at his feet would one day take God's music to the world like no one else before him. The teenaged devotee did not know it too.

I cherish that golden moment. I did not know then that destiny had already dealt its cards. Ustad Bade Ghulam Ali Khan Saheb passed away shortly after that. 26 April 1968 was one of the saddest days of my life. I had never felt so crushed at the passing away of someone whom I had not known personally. It felt like I had lost someone very dear to me. It was not just about the magnificence of his music. I had come to regard Ustad Bade Ghulam Ali Khan Saheb as my ideal. I had heard so many tales of his generosity, his humility, his personality and his devotion to music. I wanted to be like him. His passing away was a heavy blow that weighed me down for days. There was a sense of gloom.

My father felt my pain. One day, he told me, 'Great artistes don't die. They leave behind a reservoir of heritage from which impassioned souls can drink for generations and create new worlds of excellence. If he inspires you so much then get to know him more by drinking from his reservoir of music.' I decided to do that, but in life, there is a time and a place for everything. The deep dive into the ocean of Bade Ghulam Ali Khan Saheb's singing was destined to happen after a few more years. I thank God for having given me the priceless memory of that fleeting meeting at AIR, Kolkata. That memory has travelled far.

Fire

I am passion,
I am strife;
I am the spark,
I shape life;
I burn, I glow,
I harden the clay...

sa

Pandit Jnan Prakash Ghosh

Ajoy was nine-years-old when he first met Guru Pandit Jnan Prakash Ghosh. He had come to Gondolpara Jute Mill in Shyamnagar to play a *jugalbandi* (duet) with the Hindustani classical violin maestro Pandit V.G. Jog.

My Master Moshai, Guru Kanaidas Bairagi took me to meet him. I was very excited because it was my first close encounter with a classical music stalwart, and that too, not one but two of them. Guru Jnan Prakash Ghoshji said, 'Oh, so this is the boy?' and smiled. It seemed that Master Moshai had told him something about me. I touched Pandit V.G. Jog's feet too. That was in early 1962. Our next meeting, which was to become a defining moment in my life, happened after a gap of seven years.

Meanwhile as Ajoy grew up, he kept hearing about Guru Pandit Jnan Prakash Ghosh. His compositions were sought after and sung by the top-most singers of the day, including popular artistes like Hemanta Mukherjee, Manabendra Mukhopadhyaya and Sandhya Mukherjee and classical vocalists like Shrimati Manik Varma, Shrimati Tanima Thakur and Pandit Raghunath Panigrahi. He also wrote lyrics and composed music for film songs. Reports of his exploits on the harmonium and the tabla came in through Master Moshai, as also of the musical soirees that he curated or hosted. With radio being the only medium for listening to music in Ajoy's family, he also knew him as the curator of the benchmark All India Radio Kolkata music programmes, *Sangeetanjali* and *Ramyageeti*.

To say that Guru Pandit Jnan Prakash Ghosh was a genius would be an understatement. He was like the Himalayas—an almost infinite range of glittering peaks with an immeasurable spread. To see and appreciate such

a personality in all its fullness is not an easy task.

Academically speaking, Guru Pandit Jnan Prakash Ghosh was a student of the great Indian linguist Professor Suniti Kumar Chatterjee. Guru Jnan Prakash Ghosh specialised in Pali—the ancient Indian language that is home to the earliest extant Buddhist literature and was a topper in his class at Presidency College in Kolkata. He learnt painting from the great artist Abanindranath Tagore—a famous nephew of the poet-philosopher Rabindranath Tagore. Excellence in sports was another aspect of Guru Jnan Prakash Ghosh's multifaceted personality. A brilliant football player, he was also an accomplished polo, billiards and hockey player. He may have gone on to become a professional footballer had he not lost one eye in an unfortunate football-related accident. Football's loss was music's gain.

As the grandson of Dwarakanath Ghosh, the creator of the 'Dwarkin' harmonium, music was in Guru Pandit Jnan Prakash Ghosh's soul. He had never given up his childhood pursuit of music and after he gave up football, he embraced music with total surrender to move on the path that destiny seemed to be pointing at.

Under gurus like Pandit Girija Shankar, Ustad Sagir Khan and Ustad Dabir Khan for vocal music and Ustad Masit Khan (Farukhabad gharana) and Ustad Feroze Khan (Punjab gharana) for tabla, the musical sky that was dying to burst out in Guru Jnan Prakash Ghosh opened out and became his life and being. This starry sky went on to become a grand *chhatra chhaya* or sheltering shade under which many forms of music and many talented music performers bloomed. His famous tabla disciples include Pandit Kanai Dutta, Pandit Shankar Ghosh, Pandit Anindo Chatterjee, Pandit Gobindo Bose, Pandit Shyamal Bose, Pandit Nikhil Ghosh and Pandit Abhijeet Banerjee. His vocal music students include Pandit Prasun Banerjee, Shrimati Tanima Thakur, Pandit Arun Bhaduri and Shrimati Lalita Ghosh. Pandit Jnan Prakash Ghosh was also a genius on the harmonium. His renditions of ragas on the harmonium and his instrumental *jugalbandi*s are legendary. When All India Radio started National Programme of Music in July 1952, he was the first artiste to play the harmonium. Till then

All India Radio had prohibited the use of the harmonium in classical music broadcasts. A supreme musicologist and an exemplary composer, he was also a soulful vocalist and a versatile instrumentalist who could play the esraj and the piano too.

The greatest of the greats have hailed Guru Jnan Prakash Ghosh's brilliance. Even though he was honoured with the Padma Bhushan by the Government of India, posterity has not given his contribution its rightful place in India's music history. I have tried to do what I could and continue to do so. I am grateful to the West Bengal government for sanctioning the installation of a sculpture of Guru Jnan Prakash Ghosh in Rabindra Sadan in Kolkata and also for instituting the Guru Jnan Prakash Ghosh Puraskar— a state award that carries a citation and a cash endowment for excellence in the pursuit of music. But we need to do more for one of Bengal and India's greatest musical brains.

re

On 9 May 1969, about seven years since the meeting with Guru Jnan Prakash Ghosh in Shyamnagar, a news item caught Ajit Chakrabarty's eye as he opened the morning newspaper. It said that Pandit Jnan Prakash Ghosh's birthday would be celebrated in the evening, with a concert hosted by Shri Adrija Nath Mukherjee, whom they later came to know as a music patron of Kolkata.

Gurudev Rabindranath Tagore

My father called me and showed me the newspaper. 'Today is *Pouchishe Baishakh*. Pandit Jnan Prakash Ghosh shares his birthday with Gurudev Rabindranath Tagore. *Pouchishe Baishakh* means the 25th day of the month of Baishakh.' Baba smiled and said, 'Why don't we go and wish him? Everyone says that he is a very nice man. I am sure he will not mind.' My eyes sparkled. Oh, I could give anything for a visit to Kolkata and what could be better than an opportunity to meet the living legend himself—the legend from whom Master Moshai now wanted me to learn?

After lunch, Ajoy and his father started out for Hare Krishna Seth Lane in Dum Dum (the area around Kolkata airport) where Guru Pandit Jnan Prakash Ghosh lived, after shifting from his fabled ancestral home—25, Dixon Lane—which had been the venue of landmark concerts by legends like Baba Alauddin Khan, Ustad Bade Ghulam Ali Khan, Ustad Amir Khan, Pandit Ravi Shankar and many others.

We reached his Hare Krishna Seth Lane house at around 5 pm. A red Ambassador car was parked outside.

We entered, a little hesitantly, and my father rang the doorbell but no one answered. I was very disappointed. Maybe he was not at home. However, since we had come from so far, we decided to wait.

At about 7 pm, an elegantly attired gentleman opened the door and was surprised to see us. He asked us whom we wanted to meet. We got up and my father explained that we had read about the concert and had come to attend it and pay our respects to Guru Jnan Prakash Ghosh. The man asked who we were. When my father introduced himself and told him where we were coming from, the man smiled and said, 'Ajit Babu, I am really sorry that you both had to wait so long. I was not aware that you were here. Thank you for coming. I am grateful. I am Jnan Prakash Ghosh.' Then looking towards me he said, 'So, you are Ajoy... the boy that Kanai was talking about. Come in please.' His regal and yet so humble bearing was rare for a man of his stature. When we were seated, Guru Jnan Prakash Ghosh said, 'The concert is not here. It is in Sealdah at around 8.30 pm and it will go on till late in the night. I suggest that you wait for some time and then we can all go in my car'.

Sitting in Guru Jnan Prakash Ghosh's home, Ajit Chakrabarty's long struggle to give his son the perfect musical upbringing flashed before his eyes like a film in fast motion. There were artefacts and objects in the room that triggered memories of his growing up in his ancestral home in Mymensingh, a home whose comforts he had spurned to follow his passion of becoming a singer. He could not reach where his musical powers could have actually taken him. In rebuilding life from ground-zero, Ajit Chakrabarty never got the opportunity to dedicate himself to music with single-minded focus. The responsibility of fending for his family weighed heavily on his passion and he was not one who would shirk duty. The going had been tough. It still was.

Ajoy had had to suffer too. His childhood had been bereft of many little comforts and enjoyments that most children get in their growing-up years. Yet, the boy had never complained and he had followed his father's instructions to the last word. Somewhere in all this the father in Ajit Chakrabarty had to take a back seat to allow the mentor, guide and master-trainer to take charge. Today as he looked at his son there was a surge of emotions in his heart. He felt like he was sitting at the Base Camp of Mount Everest. The mountain seemed to be calling out to his son.

When it was time to leave for the concert I stepped into Guruji's red

Pandit Ajoy Chakrabarty immersed in music   *Photo courtesy: Inni Singh*

Ambassador car. He made me sit between him and my father on the back seat. It was the first of my many rides in Guruji's red Ambassador. The concert was as special as a sixtieth birthday celebration concert of a stalwart should be. Guruji performed in the end with another legendary classical music artiste—Pandit Radhika Mohan Moitra. The *Nat Bhairav* that they wove together still rings in my ears.

Ajoy knew that his Guru Kanaidas Bairagi had said more than a few good words about him to Guru Jnan Prakash Ghosh and it was also quite clear that Guru Jnan Prakash Ghosh had decided to take Ajoy under his wings. Ajoy was

excited but the human mind has a manufacturing defect. It breeds anxiety till the inevitable happens. This defect has to be worked on.

On their way back, Ajoy sat lost in his thoughts in a window seat of the last suburban train to Shyamnagar. There was so much to share with his mothers. The birthday concert in Adrija Nath Mukherjee's house was his first close encounter with classical music's heady world of patronage and praise, fans and followers. It was also a first-hand experience of the majestic magnanimity and humility that set apart truly great artistes like Guru Jnan Prakash Ghosh and Pandit Radhika Mohan Moitra.

The emptiness of the train and the darkness outside magnified the rhythmic clatter of the wheels on the rails. Dum Dum, Belgharia, Agarpara, Shodpur, Khardaha—one by one the stations went by. At each station, the train stopped to drop some passengers, pick up new ones and also gather some breath, just like we need to do in the twisting and turning journey of life.

The humble little boy of Shyamnagar was also feeling nostalgic. The gay abandon with which he was learning music, going to school, chatting up friends in the neighbourhood may not be possible, once he decided to board the train of his life at the busy junction of classical music that was now calling him.

Suddenly he felt a hand on his head. 'What are you thinking, son? Don't worry. Ma Kali will always be there to see you through. I can see you there—on the other side, behind the microphone, with hundreds of entranced listeners lost in your divine singing.' Ajoy looked at his charioteer and guide … his father Ajit Chakrabarty, who smiled and started humming one of his favourite Shyama sangeet songs. The swing of the famous kirtan seemed to blend with the rhythmic sway of the train.

Ma aachhen aar aami aachhi, Bhabnaa ki aachhe aamaar,

Aami mayer hathey khaai pori, Ma niyechhen amaar bhaar!

Mother (Ma Kali) is there and I am there. Why should I have any worry? I eat from, and am draped by, my mother's hand. My mother takes my burdens onto her.

Pore songsaar paake ghor bipaake jakhon dekhi andhokaar,
Sei ghor andhaare maa amaarey baani sonaye baarebaar.

When the coil of worldly dangers and threats darkens everything around me, my mother saves me by calling out to me all the time.

Aami bhuleo thaki tobuo dekhi bhole na maa ektibaar,
Aemon sneher aadhar ke ache, Maa je aamaar ami maar,
Baro sneher andhar maa je aamaar, aami maaer, maa aamaar.

Even if I forget my mother, my mother never forgets to remember me. There is no seat of love like my mother's. I belong to her. She is mine. She is the bedrock of love. I belong to her. She is mine.

Ajoy and his father reached Shyamnagar station. As was his habit, on reaching home Ajoy narrated everything in detail to his mothers—the journey, the meeting and the concert.

ga

Ajoy started learning formally from Guru Jnan Prakash Ghosh in July 1969.

On the first day, when he arrived in class, Guru Jnan Prakash Ghosh gave him a disarming welcome and introduced him to some of the students who had already arrived. Ajoy took his place in a corner at the back of the large room that soon filled-up with almost 50 students, including some senior performing artistes. In later years, Ajoy went on to perform with some of them. That day it was different. For some he was quite simply, a young, unassuming, newcomer from suburban Shyamnagar. For others, he was yet another mirror of their own desires to excel in the pursuit of music. For everyone he was their new *guru-bhai*, their new 'brother' in the Guruji's family.

Ajoy was poised in the reality of the situation when he took his seat in a corner of the room. He knew that struggle and strife were his credentials and passion to learn was his only visiting card. He had only one asset—his voice. He could, however, sense the buzz in the classroom when his *guru-bhai*s heard him for the first time. It was a very appreciative buzz.

Ajoy Chakrabarty, on track for a musical career

On Ajit Chakrabarty's insistence, Guru Jnan Prakash Ghosh had agreed on a fee of Rs 25 per month for being Ajoy's guru.

On most occasions Guruji returned the fee to me on some pretext or the other. The most common excuse was the 'taxi-excuse'. For example, 'I think it will rain today Ajoy. Here, keep this money. You take a taxi.' Or 'Ajoy, it has been a long day and you have an exam tomorrow. Here, keep this. Take a taxi. No, no, I insist.' As the months passed, I gathered confidence to protest more vocally, but I always lost the argument because, with each passing month, his right to command me with abounding love grew too. I got back the fee for half the year.

When one looks back on Pandit Ajoy Chakrabarty's training it is easy to see that he had been bought up in the Guru Jnan Prakash Ghosh style of training right from the outset. Providence had played its inexplicable hand. His childhood teacher, Shri Pannalal Samanta had inherited the 'Jnan Prakashi ethos' from his guru, Guru Kanaidas Bairagi, who in turn had inherited it from Guru Jnan Prakash Ghosh. Joining Guru Jnan

Prakash Ghosh's class, therefore, was like graduating within a particular school of teaching. Ajoy felt at home in the informal environment of the classroom and soaked up the free-flowing teaching. He did not find it difficult to move from one unexpected raga to another or from one genre of music to another in the course of the same class.

The monsoon was in full flow in Kolkata when Ajoy started learning from Guru Jnan Prakash Ghosh. At many places on the way from Dum Dum Station to Hare Krishna Seth Lane he had to roll up his trousers at least a few inches to negotiate puddles and pools. It rained inside the classroom too, though it was a different kind of rain. Sitting in the class was like sitting under a shower of gems. Diamond *dhrupad*s, topaz *khayal*s, emerald *dadra*s, sapphire *tappa*s, ruby-studded *thumri*s, and along with all this, many pearls of wisdom too. It was seemingly impossible to gather all the gems but only seemingly because in teaching Ajoy the dictionary of life, his father Ajit Chakrabarty had taken care to remove the word 'impossible' from it.

The class was punctuated with endless requests. If someone wanted to learn a *dhrupad*, Guruji dipped into his treasure trove, took one out and taught it. If someone followed it up with an earnest request for a *dadra*, Guruji dipped into his treasure trove again and took out yet another gem. Imagine 10, 12, 15 such gems adding sparkle to every class. I did not have a tape recorder to put the gems in a necklace of recordings and take them home. It was also very difficult to take down all the notations in such a short time in the traditional way. Those who came for a *dhrupad* here, and a *khayal* there, or a *dadra* or a *thumri* or two, took back what they wanted. I had a problem. I had a huge musical appetite, I wanted to learn everything. I wanted to take back everything. Guruji used to ask us to recall and sing what we had learnt, and it could be anything out of the treasure trove that he had shared in the previous class. Something had to be done.

A kind of a council of war was held one night. Father and son put their heads together to come up with a strategy. Ajit Chakrabarty asked, 'How does a stenographer take dictation?'

'Shorthand, Baba,' said Ajoy.

'Right, and that is what we will do!' said his father.

'Shorthand?' Ajoy asked his father, thinking that he had not heard right.

'Yes,' his father replied, 'but not the stenographer's shorthand. We will need to work out something more than the usual notation system—our own way of putting a song or composition to paper very comprehensively and very quickly.'

As an afterthought, his father asked him, 'What time does the daily Rabindra Sangeet programme start on the radio?'

Ajoy said, 'It is from 7.45 am to 8.00 am.'

Ajit Chakrabarty replied, 'That's perfect! I want you to hear the songs, write down the lyrics with the notation of each word and the transition of each note. The entire exercise has to be completed within the course of the radio programme.' From the frying pan, Ajoy had landed straight into the fire.

> It took me back to the words of my childhood poem, '*Ei daekho pencil, notebook ei haathey*', which as I have said before means something to the effect, 'Look here is my pencil, and the notebook is in this hand'. Every day, without fail, I now camped in front of the radio with a notebook and a pencil. With a hard taskmaster like my father, there was no chance of missing out on this daily ritual. Soon the ritual developed into a skill that enabled me to write down any new song along with its notations accurately and speedily.
>
> I felt like the world champion car racer of the time Jackie Stewart must have felt while negotiating a Grand Prix race track. Left turns, right turns,

U-turns, roundabouts, flyovers … I started seeing musical notes twisting, turning, pausing, gliding, accelerating, stopping and moving. Even today, I can hear and simultaneously write down the words and notations of any song instantly. It's a game I love playing. It is another matter that when I was learning to do it in front of the radio in those days, I had no idea that the Shrutinandan system of identifying and visualising notes was taking birth in me.

A few weeks later, Guru Jnan Prakash Ghosh ended up teaching as many as 17 compositions in the course of a single class. It was a stupendous task to remember them, learn them and reproduce them in the next class. Ajoy was ready with all 17 for the next class. He rendered whatever was asked. Guru Jnan Prakash Ghosh smiled because this had never happened before. He realised that in front of him was a young man whose hunger for music was as insatiable as his ability to digest the most varied and complex musical recipes.

Guru Jnan Prakash Ghosh was at heart a sportsman. He valued the spirit of the game above everything else. His approach to music was no different. He threw many tests at Ajoy. These tests were not always about music. There were tests of character, of selflessness

and of love, compassion, humility and commitment. To Pandit Jnan Prakash Ghosh, music was only as good as the goodness within the musician. His own life was a celebration of the music of human values. Whatever he touched, whatever he played, whatever he sang, whatever he taught became sublime. Ajoy's soon-to-grow, endearing, life-changing relationship with Guru Pandit Jnan Prakash Ghosh was rooted in his positive performance in these early tests. It was Guru Jnan Prakash Ghosh who put Ajoy on the highway to becoming Pandit Ajoy Chakrabarty.

Ajoy Chakrabarty was to learn from Guru Jnan Prakash Ghosh for the rest of his guru's life. This learning was not about learning through replication; it was more through realisation.

> Guru Jnan Prakash Ghosh shaped me like a potter gives shape to clay on his wheel. The wheel that Guruji set in motion is moving even today.
>
> Guruji gave me a lot more than *shiksha* or learning. He gave me *mano-deeksha*, the consecration of the mind. He also gave me a new *swara-drishti*—the ability to see musical notes in a new way.
>
> With his mind tuned to every nuance, every colour, every aspect of my voice he taught me music like a spiritual

master teaches Vedanta. It was all very subtle. He spoke a different language.

'You know Ajoy? It is very good to talk. I mean, there is nothing wrong in talking. There is also nothing wrong in adding an *alankaar* (a decorative inflection) here and there to embellish what you want to say. But it would all come to naught if we do not know how much to talk, when to talk, at what interval to talk and with how much embellishment. There has to be a sense of balance between what to convey by saying it aloud, and what to convey by leaving certain things unsaid. Have you ever realised Ajoy that we do not like to give much time to people who do not have this equanimity, no matter how good they are? Singing a raga, a *bandish* or any musical composition is also a dialogue. It is a lyrical conversation in the language of musical notes. You have to be a respectful, thoughtful, balanced talker. Otherwise, the greatest ragas and compositions will not be able to get you the desired audience response.'

This was Guruji's way of explaining how to handle a raga…

It was a bright sunny morning. There was a winter nip in the air. There were quite a few people in the class, including some senior artistes. As the class progressed, Guru Jnan Prakash Ghosh asked Ajoy,

'Have you heard Aghor Chakrabarty?'

Ajoy shook his head, he hadn't.

Guru Jnan Prakash Ghosh then asked, 'And, Ustad Abdul Karim Khan Saheb?'

Ajoy once again said no.

'What about Ustad Bade Ghulam Ali Khan?'

A little embarrassed by now, Ajoy said, 'No'.

Guru Jnan Prakash Ghosh was surprised. 'What? You have not heard Bade Ghulam Ali Khan Saheb?'

Ajoy clarified, 'I mean, I have not heard him in a live concert, Guruji. Growing up in Shyamnagar, I never got the opportunity.'

Guru Jnan Prakash Ghosh looked at him and said, 'Hmmm, you have not heard anything…'

Searching for words, Ajoy said, 'But Guruji, some of them were before my time…'

Guru Jnan Prakash Ghosh smiled and said, 'You know? It is amazing! You have not heard much compared to what most others have, and yet I want to tell you something today. Literature, mathematics, science, philosophy, art, sound, rhythm, speech … if we put it all together and look at music as a multi-

Ajoy Chakrabarty immersed in melody   *Photo courtesy: Inni Singh*

dimensional subject that demands an understanding of all this and much more, then you are the most versatile student that I have ever had.' The compliment made Ajoy's head spin.

> I did not know whether my not having heard some of the legendary musicians was more embarrassing or his praising me like this in front of everyone was. It was humbling … very humbling.

> Guruji, however, had more in store that day. He said, 'Always remember one thing—no matter how long a line you draw, someone will come someday and draw a line that is longer than yours. Then your line will be less talked of than his or her line. That is the way it is. That is the way it should be. So, draw a line that is so long that it becomes difficult, and at the same time inspirational, for someone to draw a line longer than yours. The objective is to excel more and more in such a way that not just the artiste but the art itself prospers and grows.' What he was telling me was that there is no place for pride and ego in the pursuit of art, or for that matter in pursuing any work. The words were different but the guidance was straight out of the Bhagavad Gita.

The versatility of Guru Jnan Prakash Ghosh cast its glow on his disciples in different ways. He was not just my vocal music guru. I was also privileged to learn tabla from him. He turned my aptitude for rhythm into perfection. I also learnt the art of composing and arranging music from him. When I look around and look at the history of Hindustani classical music, especially the history of the last six or seven decades, then two people come across as unparalleled gurus—Baba Alauddin Khan Saheb and Guru Jnan Prakash Ghosh. They were the devas of the *swara*—the gods of musical notes. Vast and deep like the ocean and all-embracing like the sky, they ignited the fire to excel in the hearts of innumerable disciples and devotees. Their teachings fly timelessly on the wings of time.

ma

By 1971 Ajoy was deeply grooved into the dynamic orbit of learning from Guru Jnan Prakash Ghosh. He was on the threshold of crossing his teens. Little did he know then that another twist of fate was in store for him. This twist in Ajoy's life came in the form of an invitation for his Guru Jnan Prakash Ghosh to teach in Pennsylvania University in the USA for about two years. Ajoy did not want to lose his guru. However, most of the 1970s was destined to be full of defining developments in Ajoy's life. This was just the beginning.

In hindsight, Pandit Ajoy Chakrabarty can afford more than a smile when he looks back on the decade, but the day he heard the news that Guru Jnan Prakash Ghosh would be going away for at least two years, the floor moved from under his feet. For the avid Kishore Kumar fan that Ajoy Chakrabarty was—and remains even today—it was like the great Kishore Kumar's super-hit song of the year, 'Ye kya hua, kaise hua, kab hua, kyun hua…' (What is happening? How? When? Why?), had become his own life-song. Ajoy could understand only one thing—someone sitting far away in Pennsylvania was taking his deity away.

He rang the temple bell loudly, said his prayers vociferously and raised the volume of his chants. Many of his guru-bhais did the same, but alas, his deity relocated to Pennsylvania.

There is an old proverb, 'When God points his finger He also shows the way'. Guru Jnan Prakash Ghosh raised his finger and pointed the way to a hallowed heritage that was a temple and a mosque rolled into one. Ajoy's life was about to change drastically. His dream had decided to come and stand in front of him.

One day Guru Jnan Prakash Ghosh told Ajoy, 'I have been thinking, and I have a plan for you. In my absence, I want you to learn from Munawar Ali Khan.'

The suggestion was still sinking into Ajoy's mind, when he said, 'Yes, Ustad Munawar Ali Khan, son of Bade Ghulam Ali Khan Saheb. He will be the right guru for you. He is a very nice man too. Just like his father was.'

Ajoy said, 'No Guruji, I want to continue learning from you!'

Guru Jnan Prakash Ghosh laughed, 'How can I teach you from Pennsylvania?

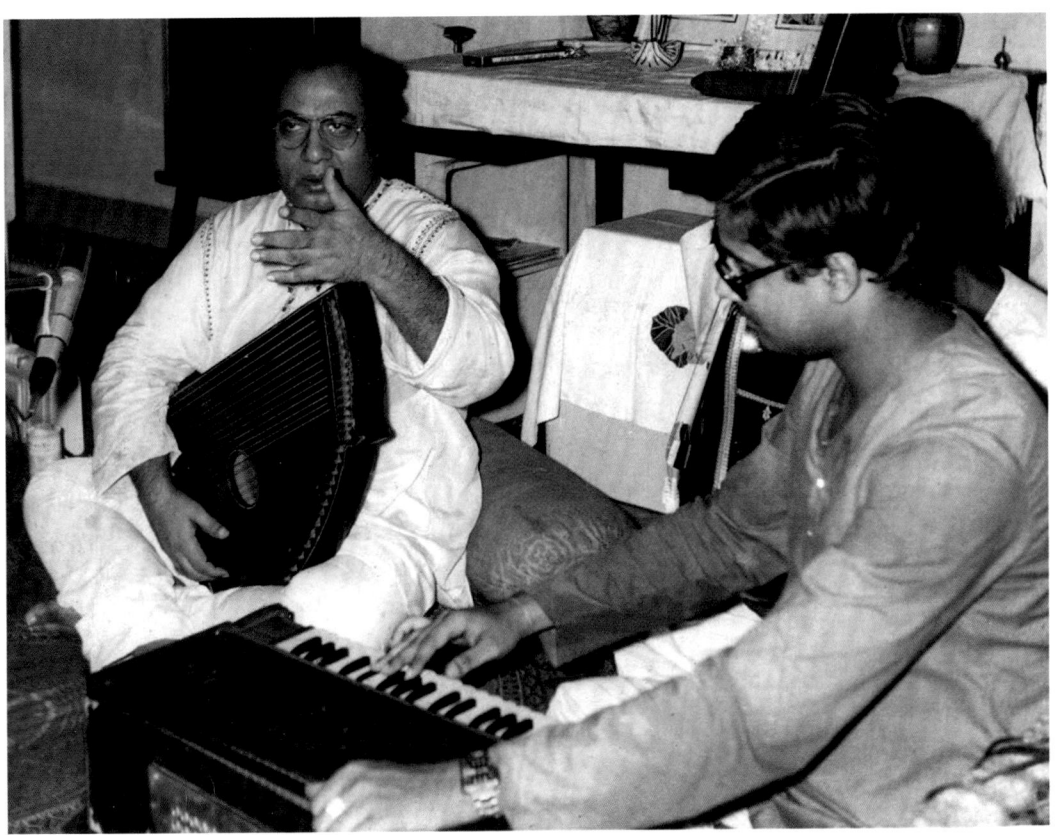

Ajoy Chakrabarty with Ustad Munawar Ali Khan

And who said that this means that you will stop being my disciple? I will be there with you as long as I live. Now trust me, and do what I say. Learning from Munawar Ali will be wonderful for you.'

Ajoy had great faith in Guru Jnan Prakash Ghosh's judgment. Brought about by unexpected circumstances Ajoy's dream was standing in front of him. Like his guru, his father Ajit Chakrabarty also asked him to embrace his dream. However, at times a question did crop up in Ajoy's mind, 'Was he losing Guru Jnan Prakash Ghosh to find Ustad Bade Ghulam Ali Khan Saheb?' And then he told himself, 'Guruji cannot be wrong about me.'

pa

They could hear the voice even as they neared the door. The voice of Ustad Bade Ghulam Ali Khan saheb. Someone was listening to a recording. The voice added to the possibilities ingrained in those moments of waiting as Ajoy and his father stood outside the door of Ustad Munawar Ali Khan's Park Circus residence in Calcutta. The *thumri* ended with a flourish. Ajoy knocked, lightly at first and then a bit louder. The door opened. They introduced themselves, after which they were ushered in and asked to wait. This was the house of the Khalifa (Caliph) of the legendary Kasur-Patiala gharana, the inheritor of the great heritage of Ustad Kale Khan, Ustad Ali Baksh Khan, Ustad Bade Ghulam Ali Khan and his younger brother Ustad Barkat Ali Khan. Mementos, awards and images, including a huge one of Ustad Bade Ghulam Ali Khan Saheb lined the walls and shelves.

This was Ajoy's first encounter with the glorious, almost fortified, concept of brotherhood that is unique to Hindustani classical music—'the gharana.' It was the antithesis of the world in which he had grown up. In the picture on the wall, Ustad Bade Ghulam Ali Khan's eyes were full of love. At one glance Ajoy knew that tales of his magnificence and magnanimity were true. Ustad Bade Ghulam Ali Khan Saheb's regal posture in the image and his signature moustache somehow seemed to suggest to Ajoy—who was feeling a little nervous anyway—that he was in for very strict learning, if Ustad Munawar Ali Khan decided to accept him as a disciple. Would he?

Soon a dignified man with his eyes full of goodness walked in. Ajoy recognised him as Ustad Munawar Ali Khan and touched his feet. Ustad Munawar Ali Khan made some general enquiries about Ajoy. On Ajit Chakrabarty's asking him if he would like to hear Ajoy before deciding to teach him, Ustad Munawar Ali Khan smiled and said, 'No. That will not be needed. Jnan Prakash Babu has recommended him. I will teach him.' Turning to Ajoy he said, 'But you may have to come every day. I hope that will not be a problem.'

'Not at all,' Ajoy replied.

I was actually quite overwhelmed by the occasion. I was entering a gharana. It was something that I had never really imagined would happen to me. I had

Ajoy Chakrabarty with Ustad Munawar Ali Khan

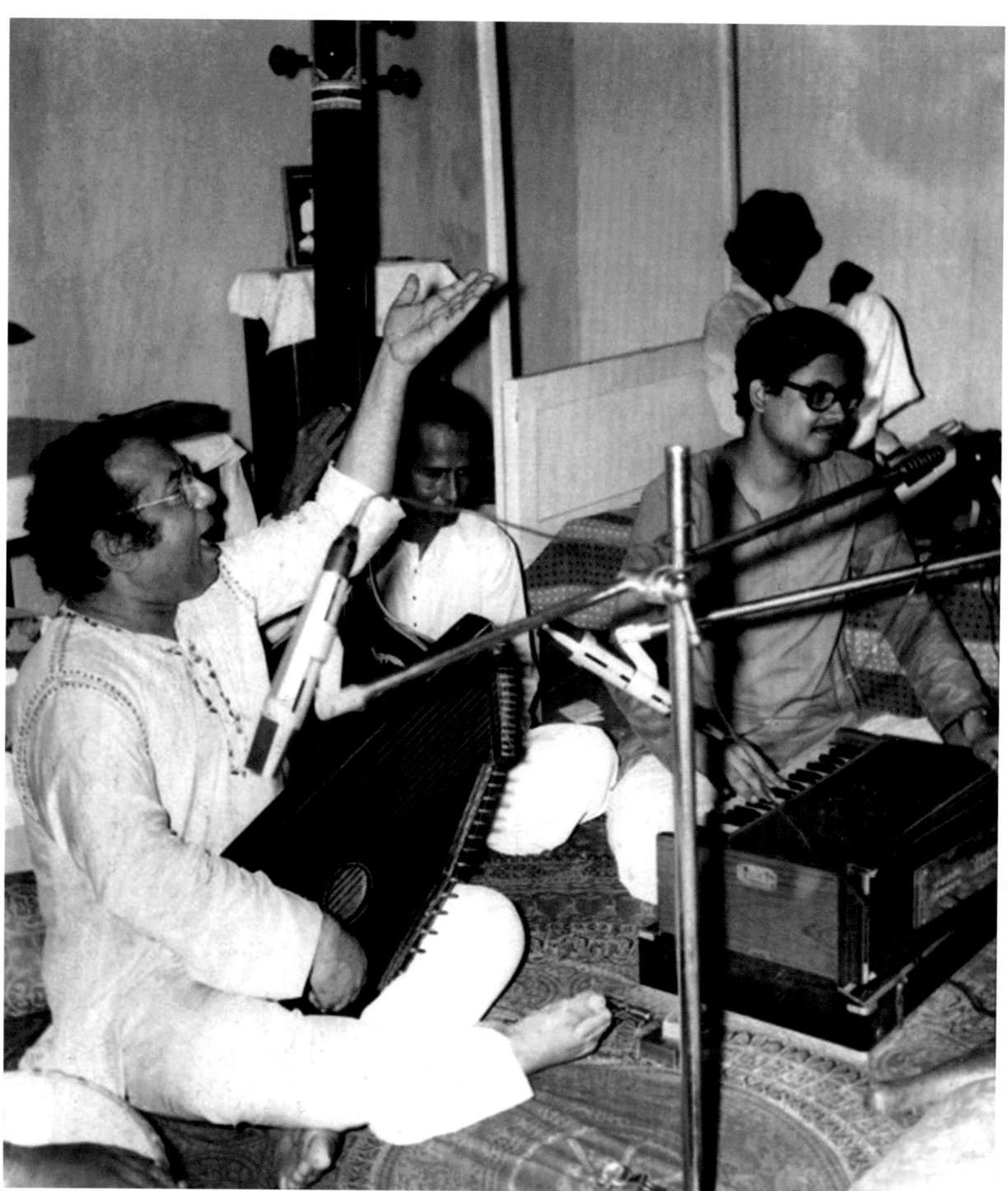

Ajoy Chakrabarty with Ustad Munawar Ali Khan during a performance

always been a very serious student of music. With a father who verged on being what I can best describe as an 'enlightened and well-meaning dictator' there was no option. Please take that lightly. I am glad that my father was what he was to me.

Anyway, here I was in Ustadji's house, entering the portals of a very formal, history-laden world of Indian classical music. Everything seemed to be rooted in *parampara* (tradition). As tradition demanded, Ustadji asked us to come the next Sunday for *ganda bandhan*—the ceremony of tying the sacred thread called *ganda*.

Ajoy's father asked Ustad Munawar Ali Khan Saheb what they needed to get for the ceremony. Ustad Munawar Ali Khan said, 'Whatever is convenient for you Chakrabarty Saheb. I have no demand, but for the ceremony get some sweets, one piece of clothing, some cotton thread and a token *nazrana*.' Ajoy and his father thanked him for his large-heartedness.

Ganda bandhan is a spiritual act that is symbolic of a divine hand-holding between the teacher and the taught. In some ways it harkens back to the ancient Upanishadic tradition of the teacher and the student chanting the shloka:

ॐ सह नाववतु ।
सह नौ भुनक्तु ।

सह वीर्यं करवाव है ।
तेजस्वि नावधी तमस्तु मा विद्विषावहै ।
ॐ शान्तिः शान्तिः शान्तिः ॥

(At the start of a class a vow to protect and nourish each other, work together energetically and study together productively, with no ill-will for each other.)

In *ganda bandhan*, a *kaleva* (a bunch of twirled red cotton threads) or any other kind of thread that may be the norm in the gharana, is generally tied to the disciple's wrist. The ceremony includes a monetary offering (*nazrana* or *dakshina*) for the ustad or guru, an offering of *shakkar* (sweets and eatables), an invocation to god and a consecration of the new relationship by what can be called an oath of allegiance and devotion on the part of the disciple and an oath of responsibility on the part of the ustad.

I made an offering of just Rs 250, a kurta and some sweets. That was the best that we could manage. A *sadhak* (worshipper) of the *swara* like his great father, Ustad Munawar Ali Khan accepted it with graciousness, tied the *ganda* and took me under his wings. He was now my Ustad (teacher) and I was now his *shagird* (disciple), Ajoy Chakrabarty.

In the gharana tradition it was expected that a student would have no other

Ajoy Chakrabarty with Pandit Jnan Prakash Ghosh

pre-occupation than *riyaaz* or practice. *Gharanedar taalim* or the gharana system of music education is about the passing on of a music house's traditions and styles. A gharana is hereditary in ethos and the basis of this heredity is the *guru-shishya* or *ustad-shagird* relationship, which is expected to be held in higher esteem than bonds of the bloodline. *Gharanedar taalim* expresses itself through the passing on of *bandish*es and *taans* as well as the manner of singing them and the gharana's distinctive ways of rendering *swara*-patterns and nuances, such as slides, glides, twists and turns, deflections and oscillations. Deviations are generally not encouraged.

This system of teaching was a paradigm shift from the way Ajoy had been learning till then. It was as if the ocean on which he had been sailing from shore to shore and port to port, was now asking him to dive deep and master the rise and fall of the tides.

In line with the belief, '*Ek saadhe sab sadhe, sab saadhe sab jaaye*' (He who masters one thing can master all but he who tries to master all loses all),

Ustad Munawar Ali Khan took Ajoy Chakrabarty across the highs and lows, the lights and shades and all the textures of one magnificent raga for the first two years—Raga Yaman. Classes were held every evening. Day in and day out, on the anvil of this spectacularly complete raga that is so challenging to conquer, Ustad Munawar Ali Khan hammered the voice of Ajoy Chakrabarty to give it the cutting-edge brilliance of a very flexible sword.

Ustad Munawar Ali Khan, or Ustadji as Ajoy called him, entrenched Ajoy's existing fascination for Ustad Bade Ghulam Ali Khan Saheb's music. The teaching of mercurial *taans* was embellished by the rhythm of narratives about Bade Ghulam Ali Khan Saheb that cropped up now and then.

Singing with Ustad Bade Ghulam Ali Khan Saheb and serving him as son and disciple, Ustad Munawar Ali Khan had been like a faithful shadow of his father, particularly in the later years of the maestro's life. In learning from Ustad Munawar Ali Khan, Ajoy was receiving the best of the Patiala heritage— the *gayaki* that had been distilled by Ustad Bade Ghulam Ali Khan Saheb and his predecessors into a fascinating pool of compositions that rippled with nuances of the *gayaki* (singing style) of Gwalior, Jaipur, Agra and Delhi that had blended into it. This pool twinkled with the reflection of many a starry *gamak, lachak, meend, ghaseet, khatka* and *murki*. It was a *gayaki* that carried the dark depths of a rain-filled monsoon cloud and the electric brilliance of thunder and lightning. It was the perfect prescription for young Ajoy. He enjoyed every bit of it and worked very hard on his training.

Ustadji's voice was very different from his father Ustad Bade Ghulam Ali Khan Saheb's voice, but then, it is not the texture of the voice but the character and temperament of the music that defines what we know as a gharana or a *baani*. I learnt my Ustad Bade Ghulam Ali Khan *gayaki* from Ustadji. Every time I heard him sing, I heard Ustad Bade Ghulam Ali Khan singing, maybe because I was always keyed on to the singing of Ustad Bade Ghulam Ali Khan Saheb.

Generally, I returned home by the last suburban train that dropped me at Shyamnagar around midnight, and at times a little after midnight too. It was a long journey and it seemed longer at the end of a tiring day. There were times when I dozed off on the train to wake up or be woken up in the yard where the train was parked.

My father would be waiting eagerly at home. He would come out of the

Pandit Ajoy Chakrabarty at a concert

mosquito net which was tucked into the sides of the bed to keep even the tiniest of mosquitoes away, although one or two always managed to get in. I guess they kept him awake for me.

Conversations generally went like, 'Got late today?' 'No Baba, just about 10 minutes late.' 'Hmmm…so, what did you learn today? Let me hear it.' My father's enthusiasm made me overcome whatever tiredness I was feeling. There was no other option anyway. My mothers' also knew that my dinner would have to wait till my so-called 'revision' or 'extra-class' got over.

My father had deep faith in my gurus. But deeper than that was my father's desire to hear me sing. He longed to hear my voice, or to be more precise he longed to hear me improve, improve and improve further. In a lighter vein, I can say that knowing that I would have to give a vocal-test for dinner at home did make me learn very attentively in class. Deep in my heart I also knew that if my biggest critic—my father—was happy with my progress, then I must be doing well. I am grateful that I did not have indulgent parents who turned a blind eye to my shortcomings.

dha

In pursuing his training under Guru Jnan Prakash Ghosh and then Ustad Munawar Ali Khan, Ajoy had not given up formal education. The year he started learning from Guru Jnan Prakash Ghosh was also the year he joined college after very good results in the Higher Secondary (school final) examination. Physics was Ajoy's favourite subject in school. His marks in the Higher Secondary examination guaranteed admission to a science course in any of the top colleges in Calcutta and Ajoy took admission in the BSc Physics course in Ramakrishna Mission College, but eventually, on the advice of Guru Jnan Prakash Ghosh, he joined the bachelor's degree course in Hindustani classical music at Rabindra Bharati University in Calcutta.

While I was learning from Ustadji I was also completing my graduation in music from Rabindra Bharati University. The two were worlds apart and they remain worlds apart even today. The university system of music education was hollow then and is hollow still. Of course, today people are giving it some thought but they are exceptions and not the rule.

I did not enjoy graduating in music even though I topped the class. First class first, as they say—ranked first with first division marks. Not that it matters much. As I look back I realise more than ever that the curriculum itself defied logic; in most universities it still defies logic.

However, on the whole graduation and the college experience helped. I must add that I was the only male student in the class. I had 30 other classmates— all girls. A few of them were serious students of music. The rest were there for reasons best known to them and their families.

During this time, Ajoy had developed another passion—he was a brilliant table tennis player who went on to become a university blue in the sport. Taking things seriously was Ajoy's childhood habit. So, he played table tennis very seriously and then, when he gave it up to focus totally on music, he gave it up very seriously too.

I have never approached anything half-way. However, in my early years, I never shut myself off from other things simply because I had to learn music. Later when I decided to make a career in classical music, I gave up the distractions and immersed myself in music. Unlike many music practitioners around me I immersed myself in all aspects of music. Does a table tennis table beckon me when I see it today? Well, frankly speaking, it always will. After all, table tennis had been one of my loves.

Can an artiste thrive on artistic prowess alone? Can any art or artiste flourish in isolation? What gives one artiste a vision that is broader than another's? What is the role of academics and education in the efflorescence of an artiste? An inspiration for young people who want to make a career in performing arts, Ajoy Chakrabarty's life provides answers to many such questions.

An academic background helps in the evolution of an artiste as a more complete individual. One who is better equipped to live in harmony with his or her art, get more out of the art and give more to the art. When one is young, the physicality of performances and presentations, accolades and encores

keep one going. As an artiste matures and his roots sink deeper, talent and expertise search for an anchor in philosophy and thinking. At this juncture, a good academic background makes a major difference. It reflects in the artiste's work and repertoire and the legacy that the artiste leaves behind.

I believe that all art is ultimately about being spiritual. Whether you have a tanpura in your hand, a sitar, a pen or cricket bat, it is the same. It is a self-exploratory journey. No one else can do this journey for you, not even your guru.

Fading away is physical excellence's inherent nature; it sometimes happens silently and sometimes all of a sudden. On these vast stretches of emptiness that are very much your own, knowledge and education can be very useful. Education enables the gushing river of talent to become an ocean of deep wonders. Education enables an artiste to understand himself or herself better and keep re-engineering his or her art. It is important because when physical gurus go away, the artiste's goal becomes his or her only guru.

Ajoy Chakrabarty appreciates the music of Ustad Bade Ghulam Ali Khan　　　*Photo courtesy: Inni Singh*

ni

After completing his graduation in 1972, Ajoy was not sure whether he should go on to get his master's degree in music or not. One of the reasons was that he knew that his father did not have money. University education would need more money. He was not a teenager any more. The fact that he was not able to share his father's financial burden troubled Ajoy, who was torn between his desire to ease the long years of suffering that his parents had endured to groom him into a singer and his desire to fulfil his parents' dream of seeing him become a successful singer. Duty called on both fronts. His father settled the issue. In a tone that closed the window on any discussion, he said, 'Get me that MA degree first'. Ajoy decided to enrol for an MA in music course at Rabindra Bharati University.

A gentleman or maybe it would be more correct to say, a person who some of us knew as a gentleman, went out of his way in offering to submit my MA admission form, along with the forms of 11 other applicants. He collected the fees from all the families. Assuring us later that the formalities for our admission had been completed, the man disappeared. Later we came to know that he had neither submitted the forms nor paid the fees. A trusting man to the core, my father was shocked. We had missed the admission dates and it was not possible to arrange for the fees again. I missed a year. Looking back, it may seem that we were very naive to have gotten into a situation like that, but that's what we really were. When I told my father that we should not have trusted the person, he said, 'Yes. But my trust in God also says that there must be some goodness in this. God can't be so unjust to us. And one more thing. Just because we have been cheated, it does not mean that we should stop trusting people.'

Ustadji—Ustad Munawar Ali Khan—did not give much importance to my not getting admission in MA. Nor did he ever object to my trying for it in the first place. Missing out on the admission for a year enabled me to focus on my tutelage under Ustadji.

In 1973 Ajoy enrolled for his masters in music from Rabindra Bharati University. Towards the end of 1974 Pandit Jnan Prakash Ghosh returned from Pennsylvania. Ajoy had been in regular

Ajoy Chakrabarty with Ustad Munawar Ali Khan

touch with him during this period. The days of emails were still far away, so he wrote letters often. When Guruji heard Ajoy on his return, he could feel the fiery confidence that had started settling in Ajoy's voice. He could see the difference that learning from Ustad Munawar Ali Khan had made. He advised Ajoy to continue his tutelage under Ustad Munawar Ali Khan. Ajoy now had the best of both worlds—imbibing Ustad Bade Ghulam Ali Khan Saheb's *gayaki*

from Ustad Munawar Ali Khan and getting insightful hand-holding from Guru Jnan Prakash Ghosh, to take it forward to a level that had never been achieved by anyone in his generation.

Ajoy had promised his father that he would complete his masters in music and he did it with record marks in 1975, topping the class yet again. This time, other than his parents he had someone else to cheer for him—a wonderful friend he had made when he joined his

MA classes, Chandana Basu. She later became Chandana Chakrabarty, Ajoy's wife and co-traveller in his quest for all-round excellence in the world of music.

The news that I along with some others had been tricked into missing our admission to MA in 1972 had done its rounds amongst the students of the music faculty of Rabindra Bharati University. Amongst them was Chandana—a wonderful soul with a very compassionate heart. We were introduced on the campus. She was in the second year of her graduation in music. Our acquaintanceship started off on a note of sympathy. ... 'Oh, you are Ajoy Chakrabarty, the boy who was duped by someone last year.' That day both of us did not have the faintest idea that this note of sympathy would grow into a lifelong raga of companionship—a companionship that gave me the strength to take on great challenges, including the challenge of setting up Shrutinandan.

The man who made me drop a year never got to know what a big favour he had done by running off with my admission money. If he hadn't, then I would not have met Chandana. As they say, every cloud has a silver lining.

While on my admission to MA, I must mention that a very noble artiste, Bengal's legendary folk singer Shri

Nirmalendu Chowdhury, who had heard of my plight, came forward to pay the admission fee, when I finally got admission for my masters in music. Even though my father paid back the money, I remain indebted to Shri Nirmalendu Chowdhury to this day. Some things can't be paid for or bought by money. Actually, the things that cannot be bought by money are the most important things in life. Later I also had the good fortune to learn some Bangla folk classics from Shri Nirmalendu Chowdhury. Maybe I should say Pandit Nirmalendu Chowdhury. Why is the title 'Pandit' or 'Ustad' reserved only for what we call classical musicians?

In university, I also found a wonderful friend in Arindam Chakrabarti, with whom I could discuss many such issues and a lot more. Spiritually inclined since his university days, Arindam became a disciple of the great Himalayan yogi Sitaram Onkarnathji. He went on to become one of the world's leading gurus of philosophy, teaching in leading institutions in the UK and USA. We shared a passion for each other's subjects then. We continue to do so after so many decades.

After completing his masters in 1975, Ajoy was once again bitten by the 'search for a job bug'. He had fulfilled his father's wish and now the road was clear to take up a job and help his father in running the household. He had seen it all—from the kirtan singing days to the kantha-sujani weaving days, the carpentry days and his father's days as a primary schoolteacher.

Ajoy was now 23 years old and was eager to shoulder not only his father's dream but also his burden. However, with a degree in music it was not easy to find a regular job. He needed to have some talent that was helpful in securing a job. Stenography! Not the kind that he had mastered in taking down notations of songs and *bandishe*s at breakneck speed but stenography and typing that could get him an office job. So, the future Pandit Ajoy Chakrabarty enrolled himself in a typing school in Shyamnagar. The young man who was destined to scale great heights as a classical vocalist and give the world a path-breaking music educational institution for children, who was to give the world the genius of his disciple-daughter Kaushiki Chakrabarty, was all set to get typecast as a type clerk.

Ajoy got himself enrolled in a typing school tucked away in a narrow lane in Shyamnagar, all set to type 'the quick brown fox jumps right over the lazy dog' over and over again. Repetition was no challenge for Ajoy. He was quite used to singing the same *taan* thousands of

Ajoy Chakrabarty with the Hindustani classical singer Smt. Hirabai Barodekar

times. This was nothing compared to that. The clitter-clatter of co-students in the little room was jarring to the ears though; the rhythm was out of sync. It was far removed from the divine swing of the clik-clak, clik-clak, clik-clak of the loom on which his father had taught him his first music lessons, by placing him on his lap when he wove sujanis. The owner of the typing school had known Ajoy for some years. There was a sympathy-laden expression on his *paan* chewing face. It was a look that said, 'See? This is what happens to people who waste time learning things like music.'

Ajoy Chakrabarty (right) playing the harmonium at a concert by Pandit Nivrutti Bua Sarnaik (centre)

Out of nowhere a job dropped into Ajoy's lap. A bank manager, who knew him to be a hardworking young man with a golden voice and a noble soul offered him a job in the bank. Ajoy did not know then that the gentleman also saw in him a prospective groom for his daughter. Very soon Ajoy had an appointment letter in his hand. He was to join on a salary of Rs 525 per month. For a young man who had grown up taking the fabric woven by his parents to sell door-to-door in Ichhapur, whose only meal at home till about the age of 14 was a *gola rooti* (a flour pancake) that sufficed as a complete meal in poor households and whose father even now earned a salary of just Rs 252 per month, it was a lot of money.

He reached home relatively early that day. When he broke the news to his father there was a tremor of sorts and then a volcanic eruption of anger. Both the quick brown fox and the lazy dog jumped out of Ajoy Chakrabarty's head and ran to dive into the holy Ganga that flowed not too far away.

Ajoy had heard the phrase 'hitting the roof in anger' and now he saw a symbolic demonstration of this. He also learnt that it is not an angry person who always hits the roof. It can also be a person who is the cause of the anger. Thankfully the roof of the room in which he showed his appointment letter to his father was a roof of tiles with a few holes in the right places.

Ajoy Chakrabarty (right) on the harmonium, accompanying Ustad Latafat Hussain Khan (centre)

I had never seen my father so angry. He tore the appointment letter and shouted, 'Have you gone mad? Is this the day I brought you up for? When you were small, people used to taunt me and your mothers. They used to say, 'Look at Ajit Chakrabarty's audacity. He does not have money to eat, and yet he wants his son to learn music.' Did we go through so many sacrifices to help you embrace the ordinary?' I tried to utter something, but the words never came out. My father continued, 'Go! Go and stand on the platform of Shyamnagar station. Watch the people coming down the stairs. Count the number of artistes you see coming down those stairs. You will be lucky if you even see one. You will see hundreds of people who are clones of each other, who work like machines in innumerable offices, trapped in their web of everyday actions … people who keep walking but reach nowhere. You want to be one amongst them? You have to be a singer and that too, not an ordinary one. I do not need such money from you. Get me just five rupees, … but there is one condition—you have to earn it with your singing. I promise I will accept it with gratitude and joy. Till then my Rs 252 per month salary will have to suffice. Do you understand?' I was taken aback. My eyes had tears. There are moments which can become tearful in a family where each one is thinking about the happiness and well-being of the other.

Young Ajoy Chakrabarty

As was his habit, his father later explained why he had felt so hurt and why he had lost his temper. Sitting in the courtyard of his house, Ajoy looked towards the *Thakur ghar* (deity's room) and vowed to never take a step back on the path! Never again! It was a Tagore-like moment, of which the great poet himself says in one of his most celebrated poems:

Klaanti aamaar kshama koro probhu,
Path e jodi pichhiye podi kabhu…

Forgive my tiredness, oh God,
If I ever fall back on my path.

Ei deenota kshama koro probhu,
Peechhon paane taakai jodi kobhu…

Forgive my poverty of strength, oh God,
If I ever glance back on my path.

By now some of Ajoy's neighbours had started wondering when he would 'settle down'. In those days and to a large extent even now, in India 'settling down' is a peculiar term used primarily for males and refers to two things: finding a job and finding a wife. Year after year, they had seen Ajoy learning music. They knew he was good at it. But still, they felt that it was time that Ajit Chakrabarty's son 'settled down'. One cannot blame them for thinking what they did. They were incapable of seeing Ajoy's parents'

vision and nor could they see Ajoy's dream and passion.

Even today most people dream ordinary dreams for their children. They encourage their children to take up extra-curricular activities but when the child stands on the brink of the pool of his or her passion, they are the first to hold the child back from plunging into the pool. Here was my father—a father extraordinary who was livid with my emotional decision to step back from the brink and stay on the shore. I dived into the pool of music. I dived like never before.

We do not know how the bank manager reacted to Ajoy's not joining his office on the appointed day. He must have been disappointed at having lost a prospective groom for his daughter. Ajoy continued learning, more immersed in his music than ever before. Classes became longer and missing a train meant that he had to sleep through the night on a bench on Sealdah Station's platform. Thankfully he was so tired that the mosquitoes could not wake him up easily. He hated the sound of the buzz though. Half asleep, he would say, 'That would be a *teevra madhyam* (F#) on the second octave of the C# scale'. He was happy as long as they were buzzing in tune.

Water

I am the river;
I am the drop;
I am the ocean,
Deep in thought;
I am a wave,
On His shore.

Top row, from left: *Gurus Ustad Bismillah Khan, Pandit Ravi Shankar, Ustad Bade Ghulam Ali Khan, Ustad Ali Akbar Khan, Pandit Ahmedjaan Thirakua and Begum Akhtar*

Middle row, from left: *Ustad Zakir Hussain, Dr M. Balamuralikrishna, Guru Gnan Prakash Ghosh, Baba Allaudin Khan, R.D. Burman and Ustad Vilayat Khan*

Bottom row, from left: *Kishore Kumar, Lata Mangeshkar, Ustad Bundu Khan, Ustad Ameer Khan, Manna Dey and Pandit D.V. Paluskar*

sa

In early 1977, Ajoy's friend Jyoti Goho, who is one of the finest harmonium players in the world today, asked Ajoy if he would like to meet his guru, Pandit A.T. Kanan. He said, 'Ajoy Da, I want to introduce you to my Guruji's music circle. It will be wonderful if you come with me. I have been talking about you. I am sure Guruji will love to meet and hear you too.'

Pandit A.T. Kanan was a highly respected name in the music world. His 'Lagi lagan pati sakhi sang' in Ritwik Ghatak's landmark film *Meghe Dhaka Tara* is as enchanting to hear today as it was in 1960, when the film released. The music circle founded by him—known as the Kolkata Music Circle—was a hub of some of the finest artistes, music lovers and music sessions in Calcutta. Ajoy agreed. He wanted to meet the man about whom he had heard so much. Everyone talked about Pandit A.T. Kanan's wonderful nature and his encouragement of young talent. There was another reason as well—the old hesitant Ajoy had ceased to exist after the bank job incident. Where he would have earlier pondered or said, 'Well, let me think about it…', he now said, 'Yes! Why not?'

Jyoti Goho asked, 'So, should I tell Guruji that that you are ready to sing too?'

Ajoy smiled and said, 'Yes! Why not?' The Sunday morning session turned out to be a milestone and the beginning of a new phase in Ajoy's life.

Ajoy put on his best clothes that morning, which is not saying much because he did not have many clothes to flaunt. The one kurta that he generally saved for special occasions came out. Attire is something that he had never paid attention to partly because he could not afford to. His finest attire and his most glittering ornament was his voice and his training and of course the blessings of his parents and his gurus.

It was an august gathering. People whose opinion mattered were there, including some well-known connoisseurs. The gathering included a man who was to become a very special person in my life, in the years to come. His name was Pandit Vijay Kichlu. He had studied *dhrupad* under the Dagar Brothers and had learnt *khayal gayaki* under Ustad Latafat Hussain Khan of the Agra gharana.

By the age of 25, I had a repertoire that was richer than that of most singers of my generation, thanks to my upbringing and my extremely diversified training under Guru Jnan

Prakash Ghosh and Ustad Munawar Ali Khan. However, I was a little nervous, though only for a few moments. I experience that nervousness even today. It is positive nervousness that puts all the senses on alert and helps in performing better. This is true of any kind of performance. It is something like what goes through a seasoned batsman's mind every time he takes his guard at the wicket before playing the first ball. While on this note, I should mention here that Pandit A.T. Kanan was a brilliant cricketer with many a winning score on the cricket field to his credit, who went on to become one of most popular classical vocalists and sought-after gurus of his time.

Jyoti Goho accompanied me on the harmonium that day. I recall that I sang *Raga Bhatiyar*.

To discerning listeners, the very first notes that a vocalist strikes can be a window that reveals a larger picture about the singer. That is exactly what happened. As Ajoy started singing, the undercurrent of appraisal and judgment soon evaporated and waves of praise and enjoyment began to rise. An impassioned young singer needs no other encouragement. Ajoy could see that the audience was moved by his singing. Remembering and thanking his gurus and mentors he ended with '*Main*

Ajoy Chakrabarty with Pandit Vijay Kichlu

to *tero naam japtaa hun*', a spritely *bandish* composed by Ustad Bade Ghulam Ali Khan Saheb with flourish. The applause was genuine.

Pandit Kanan said, 'Sing something else son'. Ajoy was not expecting this. With a nod, he said, '*Jaunpuri?*' Someone moved up from the far end of the room and said, 'Yes, *Jaunpuri*' and came and sat right in front of him. It was Pandit Vijay Kichlu. Ajoy noticed another change. Jyoti Goho had been replaced too. Pandit Sohan Lal Sharma took charge of the harmonium. This was getting more serious than Ajoy had imagined. Jyoti Goho was smiling. When Ajoy looked at him, Jyoti Goho's expression seemed to be saying, '*Jomey gaechhe, Dada! Chaliye jao!*' (*Jomey gaechhe* is an impossible to translate Bangla expression. Literally it means 'it has frozen', but actually it means just the opposite—'things are flowing.' '*Chaliye jao!*' means 'Keep it going!' and 'Dada' is the universal male salutation of Bengal. Generally addressed to an elder, it is not necessarily restricted to that. It is another Bangla word, which is almost impossible to define).

Ajoy sang *Jaunpuri* to his heart's fill. The gathering was abuzz with his rendition of '*Prabhu mohe bharosa ek tiharo*'. He was being talked of and, unknown to him, he was also being considered for a unique project. His *Bhatiyar* and *Jaunpuri* had gone a long way, and in doing so they were going to take him far. Of course, Ajoy had no inkling of what was in store. He was very happy that he had sung well and done justice to his Guruji's and Ustadji's training.

Kichlu Saheb called me and said that he and some others were going to launch a unique academy for teaching, researching and conserving Indian classical music with corporate support and that he was very keen that I should join the academy as a student. He used the word 'scholar'. In a nutshell, Kichlu Saheb shared his grand vision of what became the ITC Sangeet Research Academy or ITC-SRA. He had a vision about how scholars should learn in a modern gurukul environment with access to technical facilities, archives and guidance at every step. How each scholar would be attached to a guru and groomed into a complete classical artiste. He informed me that some of the country's leading gurus and ustads were going to be part of the academy and that I would also be attached to a guru or ustad to learn in the traditional guru-shishya mode and then launched, so to say.

I was already feeling dizzy, trying to grasp all that he was saying when he added that I would also receive a stipend of Rs 1,050 per month. I don't remember if my eyes popped out on hearing the amount but something like that must have happened! It was a stupendous amount for a poor young man who only two years back was all set to take up a 9-to-5 job at a princely salary of Rs 525. This was kingly. The scholarship was exactly double that amount. A smile broke on my lips. Kichlu Saheb must have thought it was a smile that said, 'Okay Sir I agree!' but it wasn't. What he had put on my platter was too much digest at one go. I needed some time to think.

The offer was too much to handle. The tortoise in Ajoy retreated into his protecting shell and said, 'I will have to think about it'.

'Sure,' said Pandit Vijay Kichlu, 'but don't think too much. Our Sangeet Research Academy is going to be a milestone institution. Together we can achieve so much.'

Ajoy looked at him and said, 'I am grateful that you find me worthy of this great endeavour of yours but I must discuss it with my parents and my gurus.'

Kichluji said, 'I understand, but believe me there is not much to discuss. I think your answer will be positive.' He smiled.

Ajoy said, 'Still… It is a major decision. I will get back to you.'

When Ajoy broke the news of the offer to his father, Ajit Babu's first reaction was of great happiness but that was momentary. It was like a general in the army dropping his guard for a minute, while celebrating a victory. His guard came up almost immediately. 'It sounds very good,' he said, 'but we must consider the pros and cons. This is a decision that we should not take on our own. Take time. Ask Guru Jnan Prakash Babu.'

Guruji was teaching at the Ali Akbar Khan College of Music in San Rafael, California. It was his second stint in the US. I had been missing him for quite some time. I wrote to him. His answer came by return post. The letter was punctuated with great happiness and an equal amount of amusement. He was very happy that I had received such an offer. He was amused that I had written to him for advice and permission. He wrote, 'Is this something that one should have second thoughts about? Does anyone ask for permission to take up such an opportunity? Only you can think of doing so. You must join!'

Ajoy wanted one last assurance. He wrote to Guru Jnan Prakash Ghosh that he would take up Kichlu Saheb's offer only if Guru Jnan Prakash Ghosh promised

that he would not stop teaching Ajoy. Guru Jnan Prakash Ghosh assured Ajoy that gurus were for all times.

But I still needed Ustadji's permission. When I first briefed him about the offer he said no. He advised me against taking it up. He believed that there was no need for it and that I should continue to learn the way I was learning. He was a very simple man who had genuine faith in the gharana system of training. The whole concept of the ITC Sangeet Research Academy—which remains revolutionary to this day—must have sounded very unsettling to the traditionalist in Ustadji. I understood and appreciated his feelings. He had my welfare in mind.

I was very sure that I would not join ITC-SRA if I did not get permission from Ustadji. I decided to bring up the subject again. I genuinely believed that in joining ITC-SRA I would not only be able to represent the Kasur-Patiala heritage but also do research on it. I opened my heart out to Ustadji. I had

already promised him that I would join ITC-SRA only if they allowed me to continue learning from him. Ustadji said that he wanted more time to think. After a few days, he gave me his blessings and his permission to join ITC-SRA as his disciple. I remain indebted to him. He took time to think but only to place my interest and welfare before anything else.

I then approached Kichlu Saheb with two clauses. Clause one—that I would not stop learning from Guru Jnan Prakash Ghosh. Clause two—that I would not stop learning from Ustad Munawar Ali Khan.

Pandit Vijay Kichlu's dream was founded on his vision of nurturing and conserving the gharana system and the gurukul tradition in which an artiste is groomed to take forward the *gayaki* of a gharana by staying with and learning from a leading guru or ustad of that gharana. However, Pandit Kichlu now had a predicament— of starting his dream project with a scholar who did not want to be attached to any particular guru in the proposed academy. Pandit Vijay Kichlu, who was a devoted admirer of Ustad Bade Ghulam Ali Khan Saheb as well as Ustad Faiyyaz Khan's *gayaki* did not want to lose this brilliant youngster. It was Ajoy's passion for reliving Ustad Bade Ghulam Ali Khan Saheb's *gayaki* that had been one of the reasons why he wanted to have Ajoy in the academy. Pandit Vijay Kichlu had some quick thinking to do. Ajoy, on his part, was sure of his decision.

I was absolutely sure of my stand. I told Kichlu Saheb, 'I don't think there is a better guru for me than Pandit Jnan Prakash Ghosh and Ustad Munawar Ali Khan. I am learning from them. I am here, in front of you, because of what they have taught me. I will join your academy but also continue to learn outside the academy from my Guruji and Ustadji.' Kichlu Saheb looked at me very thoughtfully and agreed!

Ajoy Chakrabarty became the first scholar of ITC Sangeet Research Academy. Till the time of writing this book, he remains the only scholar who was allowed not to be attached to a particular guru.

re

Ajoy Chakrabarty joined ITC Sangeet Research Academy in March 1978. Formed in 1977, the ITC Sangeet Research Academy had grown out of the great popularity of ITC sangeet sammelans, which had captured the imagination of classical music lovers in the country, since they were first launched in 1971. With impassioned people like Pandit Vijay Kichlu at the helm, these concerts transcreated ITC Limited's vision of conserving and nurturing the great heritage of Hindustani classical music by establishing a unique learning institute for classical music. Its formation was talked about; its creation was news. And as its first hand-picked scholar, Ajoy Chakrabarty became talked about too.

> Joining the ITC Sangeet Research Academy made an immediate difference to my identity. Frankly speaking, I had no unique identity before joining it. I did not belong to a known music family. I was not from Kolkata. I was just one of the many talented aspirants in the world of Hindustani classical music. My gurus were my only 'parichay' or introduction. I was extremely proud of that introduction though. Guru Jnan Prakash Ghosh and Ustad Munawar Ali Khan were huge names. But now, for the first time in my life, I had an introduction that sounded more like my own ... the first scholar of ITC Sangeet Research Academy. It was an introduction that gave joy to my gurus. They had given me so much and I had hardly given them anything in return. Now, at least I could give them a sense of satisfaction that their training had found recognition. Back home in Shyamnagar it was easier for my parents to explain my credentials to some people who had given up on Ajit Chakrabarty's singer-son Ajoy having a worthwhile future of any kind. And Chandana ... well, now she could also give a more confident picture about me to her family. I have many more reasons to feel indebted to ITC and the ITC Sangeet Research Academy.

Ajoy Chakrabarty's not being attached to a particular guru at ITC Sangeet Research Academy made a huge impact on his evolution as an artiste. He could learn from anyone anytime. And so, while continuing his training under Ustad Munawar Ali Khan and Guru Jnan Prakash Ghosh when he returned

Ajoy Chakrabarty

to India, Ajoy Chakrabarty also started picking up valuable lessons from gurus like Pandit Nivrittibua Sarnaik, Ustad Nissar Husain Khan Saheb, Pandit A.T. Kanan, Vidushi Hirabai Barodekar, Ustad Latafat Hussain Khan, Ustad Yunus Khan and others.

Soon after joining ITC-SRA in 1978, Ajoy got a chance to perform on stage. It worked like an elixir for his soul. He gave six vocal performances in ITC sangeet sammelans and accompanied senior artistes on the harmonium on three occasions. He earned Rs 9,000 for these appearances. This was over and above the monthly stipend that he received. Ajoy had not forgotten that his father had once told him, 'Get me just five rupees ... but there is one condition— you have to earn it with your singing.' He had put his first stipend in his father's hands with great joy. As far as the Rs 9,000 windfall was concerned, Goddess Lakshmi, the Hindu deity of wealth and prosperity, knew that this

Students of the ITC Sangeet Research Academy,
Ajoy Chakrabarty and Rashid Khan

making their disciples practice one small *taan* a thousand times. This was a very different *riyaaz*. It was almost physical. He marvelled at the disciples repeating and practising the same thing for 10 to 12 hours every day. It was a ritual like the relentless chant of a Sufi *faqir*. Ajoy bowed his head to the essence of what he was seeing—to the hard fact that a singer cannot win on the strength of knowledge and passion alone and that intelligence cannot compensate for vocal endurance and discipline. He realised that it was very important to physically exercise the voice to make it a durable vehicle for sharing one's art with the world for a long time.

money was soon going to be put to very good use. Soon. Very soon!

Practice makes an artiste perfect. Intelligence sets the artiste apart. The second alas, is of no value without the first. A great impact of joining ITC Sangeet Research Academy was that it exposed Ajoy to a world of *taleem* or training that he had not really seen before. All these years he had been practising everyday—as much as his tough schedule allowed. At ITC Sangeet Research Academy he saw ustads

Ajoy started practising like never before—for 12 to 14 hours a day, six days a week. The seventh day—Sunday—was generally reserved for the home front. Things were happening on that front too. Ajoy Chakrabarty's roller-coaster decade—the 1970s—had more in store for him. Something that was to use the Rs 9,000 that he had earned from his first concerts with ITC Sangeet Research Academy—marriage.

ga

Ajoy Chakrabarty married Chandana Basu in 1979. It was what both Ajoy and Chandana wanted, but it was what in India is called an 'arranged marriage'—a marriage officially initiated and blessed by both families. The concern and admiration that Ajoy and Chandana had for each other became a binding knot of togetherness between them. Chandana became an incredible source of inspiration and support for Ajoy. An excellent vocalist herself, she had completed her masters in music in 1977 from Rabindra Bharati University securing the first position in her class.

The way Ajoy was singing in the 1970s, made it amply clear that he was a notch above the rest. Perceptive and farsighted, Chandana realised very soon that of the two, he was the more accomplished singer. Even before marriage, Chandana had started dreaming the dreams of the Chakrabarty household—of Ajoy rising to great heights in the world of music. She admired Ajoy Chakrabarty for his vocal excellence and musical knowledge but she was drawn to him because of his simple, trusting and uncomplicated nature. In Chandana, Ajoy found

Chandana Basu, as a bride

someone in front of whom he could open his heart and soul with total trust. He also found in her a treasure trove of very sensible advice.

In marrying Ajoy Chakrabarty, Chandana became the wind in the sail of his talent. Right from the outset she knew and accepted that she would have to make many sacrifices. She never stepped back from making them.

Both Ajoy and Chandana were mature individuals when they decided to marry.

Chandana Basu Chakrabarty on her marriage day

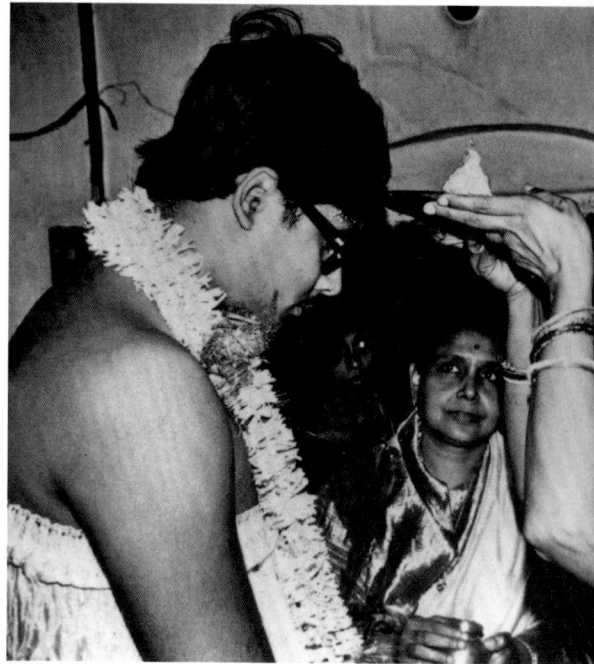

Ajoy Chakrabarty receives blessings from his mother-in-law Smt Geeta Basu

Ajoy was 27, Chandana was 24. They understood that in an artiste's life the chances of the boat docking on the cons side of the shore was always a distinct possibility. If Ajoy had confidence, then Chandana had something more—confidence and faith. She was absolutely sure that she could create a world of love, harmony and happiness using the modest stipend that her husband

received. She also knew that music would always be Ajoy Chakrabarty's first love and long hours of all-forgetting, all-effacing *riyaaz* would be his closest companion for the next few years. Chandana embraced the truth. Ajoy never forgot that embrace.

> From the very first day, Chandana became the greatest support of my life and my dreams. My father had always been my best advisor. My mothers' showered me with love. But here was someone whose smile erased all my worries. My difficult journey now had a companion. That is an incomparable blessing on the journey of life.

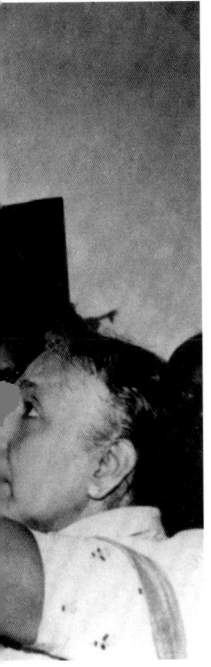

*Ajoy Chakrabarty with his father-in-law Shri Anil Krishna Basu and
father Ajit Chakrabarty during his marriage ceremony*

Soon after our marriage, I had to shift my residence to Aldeen, the heritage complex in Tollygunge that houses ITC Sangeet Research Academy even today. I was allotted scholar-accommodation at the Academy.

I had a dream for Chandana too. She was a brilliant singer. I wanted her to continue singing and reach the pinnacle of success and recognition as a vocalist. Chandana, however, took a different call. She decided to stay back in my Shyamnagar home to take care of my parents, while I shifted to Aldeen. That was a huge sacrifice. She made it so that I could settle down in my new world and learn without worries. Once a week, I went home to Shyamnagar. Partings were tough for both of us. She not only understood but reminded me, lest I forget, that I was in a very crucial stage of my career and that I could not afford to let go of the *laya* or tempo that had been set.

Chandana knew that Ajoy Chakrabarty was living life under the lens. She knew that her husband's progress was being scrutinised not only by those who had given him an opportunity to be a part of the ITC Sangeet Research Academy, but also those who felt that musical

Ajoy and Chandana Chakrabarty during their wedding ceremony

talent could only prosper in a traditional gharana environment. She wanted Ajoy to prove many a point to the world. The singer in Chandana took a back seat and she focused on backing Ajoy. It made all the difference in Ajoy Chakrabarty's life. Chandana kept up her *riyaaz* though. Music remained Chandana's world in many ways, in particular the music of the man she loved.

> Chandana means so much to me. In a lighter vein, I now sometimes tell her that she is my mother too—like she is 'Guru Ma' to the students of Shrutinandan. She may take it as

a joke, but the fact remains that I have learnt a lot from her. Today she is the backbone of Shrutinandan. I have been able to travel and perform worldwide, because deep in my heart I know that Chandana is there to look after our world.

Success is a gift that we give ourselves with the hard work that we put into developing the potential that we have. No one can push anyone into becoming successful, because success is an inward journey that one has to eventually undertake on the strength of one's own merits and commitments.

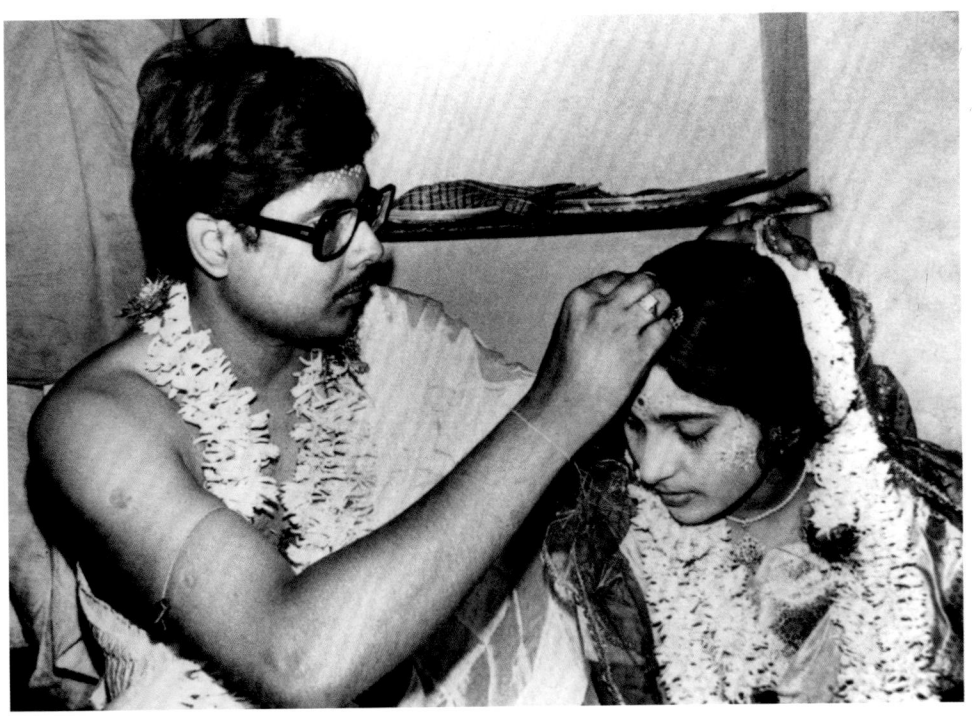

Ajoy and Chandana Chakrabarty begin their journey as a married couple

Ajoy and Chandana Chakrabarty offer their respects to Bade Ghulam Ali Khan

Ajoy and Chandana Chakrabarty with elders—Ajit Chakrabarty, Raichand Baral and Chinmoy Lahiri

Ajoy and Chandana Chakrabarty with guests at their wedding reception. From left:
Ajoy Chakrabarty's father Ajit Chakrabarty, (A) Gufam Premesh Ghosh, (B) Khadim Hussain Khan
(C) Vishar Hussain Khan (D) Buddhadev Dasgupta (E) Latafat Hussain Khan, (F) A.T. Kanan
(G) Smt. Girija Devi, (H) Smt. Hirabai Barodekar

ma

Life had placed the shy, young, music-worshipping boy of Shyamnagar on a track whose rhythm was punctuated with many new patterns and whose tempo was much faster than what he had earlier been used to. An ITC Sangeet Research Academy scholar, a rising star and a double-disciple with a much greater responsibility on his shoulders, Ajoy now had a lot more to think about. His mind needed an anchor. In such times, a true artiste always turns to his art. For Ajoy too, *riyaaz* provided the answers. Relentless practice became the *sthyaai* (signature) of the *khayal* of Ajoy Chakrabarty's life. He took a solid grip on the benchmark that he had set for himself. On the slate of his mind he had already scribbled the number 84—the number of hours that he would try to practice every week. From 1978 to 1985, even with growing responsibilities at home, at ITC Sangeet Research Academy and in the performing world, Ajoy Chakrabarty never compromised with his target of 84 hours of practice. At the same time, he continued exploring different strains of Hindustani classical music, the deeper philosophies of *raga sangeet* and the music of the world.

I joined ITC Sangeet Research Academy at a time when the academy was in the teething stages and was coming to terms with its rules, regulations, norms and conventions. After joining the ITC Sangeet Research Academy, I took up some concert offers outside the academy. It was nothing major, but Kichlu Saheb did not like it and he was frank in telling me so.

I had great respect for both Kichlu Saheb and the ITC Sangeet Research Academy and so there was no question of disagreement. Anyway, I was not the only one to have done so. These happenings led the ITC Sangeet Research Academy to come up with the idea of a 'bond' in 1980. Kichlu Saheb decided that scholars should sign a 10-year bond with the ITC Sangeet Research Academy. This was understandable because ITC was investing so much in our growth. I was asked to sign a 10-year bond too.

Ajoy Chakrabarty may have been a little unsure about signing the bond, but his father had no doubts. When Ajoy reached home in the evening and told his father about the bond, Ajit Chakrabarty said that they would discuss it in the morning. Next morning as they sipped their tea in the courtyard, Ajit Chakrabarty said, 'I have been thinking about it. Resign.'

Ajoy looked at him, not sure whether he had heard right.

Ajit Chakrabarty again said, 'Yes resign. The stipend is not the deciding factor. So, don't worry about that. An artiste needs to be free, not bound. You will not sign a 10-year bond. Leave the ITC Sangeet Research Academy if need be.'

Ajoy looked at his father again. Ajit Chakrabarty still earned only a few hundred rupees a month. Yet, he was prepared to give up the attraction of the ITC Sangeet Research Academy's stipend in his son's interests. That day Ajoy learnt the lesson of fearlessness from his father once again. His mind went back 11 years earlier to the train journey from Sealdah to Shyamnagar, while returning from Guru Jnan Prakash Ghosh's 60th birthday concert. He looked towards the *Thakur ghar*. The song came back to his ears...

Maa aachhen aar aami aachhi, Bhabnaa ki aachhe aamaar,
Aami mayer hathey khaai pori, Maa niyechhen amaar bhaar!'

Mother (Ma Kali) is there and I am there. Why should I have any worry? I eat

from, and am draped by my mother's hand. My mother takes my burdens onto herself.

Ajoy went back and communicated his family's decision to Pandit Vijay Kichlu. Panditji tried to reason with him. Finally, after many more discussions, a 2-year bond was agreed upon between the ITC Sangeet Research Academy and Ajoy Chakrabarty.

I was then appointed a 'musician scholar'. It was a promotion of sorts from being an ordinary scholar. My stipend of Rs 1,050 remained the same. With my two-year bond I stayed on to bond eternally with Pandit Vijay Kichlu's dream and ITC Company Limited's vision and commitment. After so many years I think that I have vindicated the stand that I took that day by not signing the 10-year bond. Some relationships are not dependent on a signature on a piece of paper. They are signed on the unseen stamp paper of the soul.

Identities grow. New impressions get imprinted on older ones even as some old impressions fade away. This was just the beginning. Ajoy Chakrabarty was on his way to creating a unique identity in the world of music. Towards the end of 1982 Ajoy Chakrabarty was given a student.

Ajoy and Chandana Chakrabarty

Though I was given a student, I still remained a musician scholar. But it was a threshold moment in life … I had been considered worthy of being able to teach. It was a wonderful feeling.

I had by now become an intrinsic part of the ITC Sangeet Research Academy's family and the wondrous world of Aldeen. I still had a lot to prove to myself and to the world around me. I still followed my 84 hours a week *riyaaz* target diligently.

pa

Ajoy and Chandana Chakrabarty with Manna Dey and friends

There is a parallel story in Ajoy Chakrabarty's multifaceted growth after he joined ITC SRA—the story of Ajoy Chakrabarty's mastering of the fabulous *gayaki* of Ustad Bade Ghulam Ali Khan Saheb.

In venturing into the hallowed world of Ustad Bade Ghulam Ali Khan's *gayaki*, Ajoy Chakrabarty was venturing into a world where seasoned artistes feared to tread. However, the attraction for him was magnetic and its pull irresistible. It must have been the pull of some past life. In his epic poem *Aag ki bheekh* (Alms of fire) the great Hindi poet Ramdhari Singh 'Dinkar' says, '*Aakash par anal se likh do adrisht mera*' (write the unseen—my future—with fire, on the sky). In asking to be the beholder of Ustad Bade Ghulam Ali Khan's heritage, Ajoy Chakrabarty was asking for the *bhiksha* (alms) of fire. And God gave it to him.

The desire to hold Ustad Bade Ghulam Ali Khan's music in your throat is akin to a desire for grasping fire. It can burn the

Ajoy and Chandana Chakrabarty with Guriji and family, Lalita Ghosh (rear row, second from right) and Arun Bhaduri (front row, second from right) and family

beholder to ashes if it is not held well. Many expected the young man to burn out. There were those who felt that it was audacious for a rank outsider like Ajoy to think of walking this fiery path. But these were people who did not know Ajoy Chakrabarty and his dedication well enough.

Perhaps the Carnatic music term *baani* (voice or vocal style) would be more appropriate in describing Ajoy Chakrabarty's association with Ustad Bade Ghulam Ali Khan Saheb's *gayaki* than the Hindustani classical music term gharana (familial tradition). Ajoy's world revolved around his ideal's *baani*. For him, Ustad Bade Ghulam Ali Khan's *baani* was both a parent and a child

of the gharana. Gharanas wither away but their *baani*s live on. *Baani*s never die. They take on new colours, new names. Ajoy Chakrabarty wanted to emulate Ustad Bade Ghulam Ali Khan Saheb's singing and share it with the world as best as he could. He dipped into the reservoir of research on Ustad Bade Ghulam Ali Khan from about 1980 to 1984.

Ustad Bade Ghulam Ali Khan composed *bandishes* using the pen-name 'Sabrang', literally meaning 'all-colourful'. *Khayal, thumri, dadra, tappa, bhajan* … I wanted to colour myself in all the colours of his music. As agreed to with the ITC Sangeet Research Academy I continued to learn from Ustad Munawar Ali Khan. At ITC-SRA, I also had access to rare recordings of Ustad Bade Ghulam Ali Khan. Pandit Vijay Kichlu ensured that I got everything that would enable me to go deep into the study of Ustad Bade Ghulam Ali Khan's *gayaki*. That wasn't all. As a scholar of ITC Sangeet Research Academy I got invaluable insights into the *gayaki* of Ustad Bade Ghulam Ali Khan Saheb from gurus like Ustad Fahimuddin Dagar, Ustad Umar Khan, Ustad Yunus Hussain Khan, Pandit A. Kanan and Vidushi Malavika Kanan besides Kichlu Saheb. They turned the practitioner in me into a man on a many-coloured 'sabrangi' quest! For over three years I studied Ustad Bade Ghulam Ali Khan's *gayaki* like a scientist researches a phenomenon. It was a microscopic study. The fact that I was not directly learning from him, but from people who knew him best, also worked to my advantage because it allowed me to be both analytical and experimental.

It was while listening to Ustad Bade Ghulam Ali Khan Saheb day in and day out that I realised that he was very different from most others because he exposed the alphabets of music—the 12 notes—replete with their correct placements like a bud unfolds its petals, while a majority plunge into the ocean of instant creativity while singing a raga.

Ajoy Chakrabarty knew that he would attract comparisons and even criticism on many fronts. He had no misgivings about himself—he was not trying to copy anyone. Neither was he out to compete with anyone. So, the fear of comparisons never played on his mind. There was another factor at play though. While on the one hand, Ajoy was learning from none other than the son and music inheritor of the great maestro, on the other he was also the disciple of a guru like Pandit Jnan Prakash Ghosh, who in spite of being an ardent admirer and a dear friend of Ustad Bade Ghulam Ali Khan Saheb was the antithesis of the gharana system. Ajoy Chakrabarty's approach to learning Ustad Bade Ghulam Ali Khan's *gayaki* was thus different from others who had learnt in the typical mould of the gharana.

Ustad Munawar Ali Khan gave me bountifully with open hands. Guru Jnan Prakash Ghosh also gave me bountifully but insisted on my receiving the bounty with an open mind. From Ustad Munawar Ali Khan Saheb I learnt reverence for tradition. From Guru Jnan Prakash Ghosh I inculcated freedom of expression and innovation. I could not have asked for a better combination.

dha

Ajoy Chakrabarty learnt music in what can be called the 'Age of Generosity'. Guru Jnan Prakash Ghosh took him under his wings. He had no qualms about sending him to Ustad Munawar Ali Khan. When Guru Jnan Prakash Ghosh returned to India after his first stint in the US, Ustad Munawar Ali Khan had no problem with Pandit Ajoy Chakrabarty learning from both of them. At the same time, Guru Jnan Prakash Ghosh was also very magnanimous in insisting that Ajoy Chakrabarty learn Raga *Barwa* from Ustad Latafat Hussain Khan of the Agra gharana or Raga *Nand* from Vidushi Hirabai Barodekar because they were the finest exponents of these ragas in their time. Ustad Latafat Hussain Khan Saheb and Vidushi Hirabai Barodekar were equally generous in teaching these ragas as and when the opportunity arose. Pandit Ajoy Chakrabarty said,

Ajoy and Chandana Chakrabarty practising music with Samar Saha

'A guru is someone who is not just a technical teacher; he also teaches the philosophy behind the music you create. Ultimate learning comes from within. If you can't follow your master's philosophy and imbibe it, it's useless to try and learn it at all.'

Guru Jnan Prakash Ghosh was the epitome of creativity—highly passionate and highly involved in his creation when creating it but absolutely non-possessive about it when he gave it away to an artiste. For him music was about going deep, enjoying the dive and then surfacing to dive somewhere else and coming up with something new. Newness and the constant search for it within the folds of the old was his way of being.

Guru Jnan Prakash Ghosh was a musician with a tremendously analytical mind. It was fascinating to watch him compose a song. He gave immense thought to what the raga should be, what the 'chalan' or progression of the song should be and also how it should be sung. He was in total control of his creation but never possessive about it. After composing something he let go of it. He was also always open to learning.

One day he taught me a composition. When I sang it for him after learning it, he said, 'You have sung it so well that it has raised the level of my composition. It sounds really good.' That was his way of teaching. Such praise was not reserved for me alone. Guruji praised his students openly. He would say, 'You must think how you will sing it. There is no need to sing it like me. I would like to hear how you can do something new with what I am teaching.' When I improvised on his structure he was very happy. He enjoyed listening to his students.

Ustad Munawar Ali Khan was a study in contrast. He was a picture of patience. It was another world—a world in which immersion in raga sangeet was about preserving traditions. A disciple was expected to grasp the finest details and render them to sound as close to the original as possible.

Ustadji was a perfectionist. Guru Jnan Prakash Ghosh was also a perfectionist but in a totally different way. Ustadji kept correcting me till I got the phrase

Ajoy Chakrabarty in concert

or the *taan* the way he believed it should be rendered. Like a father, he explained, '*Suno beta, dhyan se suno main kaise bol raha hun. Is tarah bolo. Ye sahi andaaz hai*' (Son, listen carefully to how I am singing it. This is the way it should be rendered). I gained a lot from this 'Follow the Ustad' system too.

Both Guruji and Ustadji were very knowledgeable and uncompromising while teaching. One expected me to experiment and the other expected me to attain perfection. What can be a more productive combination? In the end I think they were both satisfied.

That, however, was not all. Ajoy Chakrabarty had a very insightful guru in Shyamnagar too. He may not have learnt music formally like his other gurus, but this guru knew something much better than any of Ajoy's other gurus.

He knew Ajoy Chakrabarty like the back of his hand. He knew everything about him. He knew till what level of perfection Ajoy Chakrabarty could reach and what standards he could set, better than anyone else. To have someone like this with you makes so much of a difference. Such people remain unsung. In fact, their desire to see someone they love becoming successful is so intense that they are not bothered about how much attention they themselves get or what people think about them.

I remember reaching home and my father saying, 'Oh, so you recorded Malkauns? *Mandir dekh dare* Sudama? Very good. Bring the tape recorders.'

By now, we had two small tape recorders. On one he played my recording and on the other Ustad Bade Ghulam Ali Khan Saheb's recording. It was a fearsome situation for me.

The tapes were played in turn, mostly bit by bit. Stop! Rewind! Play! Clik! Clak! Clik! Stop! Rewind! Play! Clik! Clak! Clik! The sounds were familiar. They sounded like the 'clik clak' of the loom on which Ajit Chakrabarty wove the sujanis, while teaching Ajoy the seven notes in his childhood. The child was now a scholar at ITC Sangeet Research Academy but that hardly mattered to father or son. Playing a phrase again and again, Ajit Chakrabarty would say, 'See? You can do much better here. I am not saying that you have sung wrong. But I know you can do much better—more like Ustad Bade Ghulam Ali Khan Saheb. Yes. In this part! See how he presents this phrase. You missed the little inflection on the *komal rishabh*. It is the beauty of this phrase. Work on it. Do it your way … but do it.'

Pandit Ajoy Chakrabarty said, 'I did not know whether to be embarrassed by the comparison or feel happy that I was being compared to Ustad Bade Ghulam Ali Khan Saheb. It unnerved me but made me work harder. In my heart, I knew that my father was right.'

The synthesis of tradition, inheritance and individuality in Ajoy Chakrabarty's singing was best described by Guru Jnan Prakash Ghosh when he said, 'Ajoy's *gayaki* and his rendition of the Kasur-Patiala gharana repertoire is unique because he blends the *laalitya* (grace and beauty) of Bengal with the *alankaran* (adornment and glitter) of Punjab. The result is so beautiful.'

I cannot forget a concert in Delhi in 1982. Ustadji was in the audience. I sang *Yaman*, the raga that Ustadji had ingrained in my soul so lovingly over a period of two years. Eminent musicologist and music critic Shri Prakash Wadehraji was also there and heaped his compliments on me. What made the evening unforgettable was my Ustadji's words. He said, 'Even though he taught so many people, my father was unfortunate not to have had a disciple like you. I, on the other hand, am so lucky to have you as a disciple. May God bless you!' It takes a lot of magnanimity for a guru to say this about his disciple. Ustadji was a truly great human being.

ni

Knowledge has no meaning if it is not internalised. Only knowledge that becomes a disciple's own experience can carry a disciple far and do justice to a guru's teachings. This assimilation of imparted knowledge has to be done in a way that a disciple can express it best. Replication cannot be the end. It can only be a means to the end. No disciple who is a clone of his teacher reaches very far. Only thinking-artistes become great artistes—in any field of art. Hindustani classical music, by its very nature, offers room for imagination, improvisation and individualistic expressions. It has travelled so far over the centuries because in receiving, repeating and imbibing form, intonation and content some very inspired musicians have enriched it from time to time by their own thinking. The history of music is, in part, the biography of inspired individuals. The other part is the biography of inspired patrons.

What do we mean when we say 'voice'? What makes a voice, 'a voice'? What does the uniqueness of a voice consist of? What does this mean in the ordinary sense of the word? Breath, tone, pitch, scanning, inflection, accent, throw, texture—physically speaking all these go into creating the aural or audible form of a voice. Is that all? Is there a psychological element that adds to or subtracts from all this? While all these elements combine to make each voice unique, they can also be combined to make a voice sound like someone else's. The probability of such a thing happening is very high if a disciple learns in a copy-paste mode without using his or her mind or without singing to his or her soul. The mind is the most important element that goes into creating a voice. Only such a voice has a soul that is very much its own.

Initially I sang exactly like my Ustadji. Maybe whenever I sang, my reverence for him imprinted his image on my mind and his intonation got imprinted on my voice. I remember replicating him. My father made me realise this. He reacted very strongly on such occasions. 'Just a minute! Where is your voice? I want to hear Ajoy Chakrabarty singing. You remember Ajoy Chakrabarty? Or have you forgotten him? Tell me. Do you eat the same diet as Ustadji? Biryani, korma and kebabs? Do you copy his hairstyle? Do you dress like him? Food, history, experiences … Everything about both of you is different. So how can the voice be the same? Why should it be? Why are you copying him, even if unconsciously? All right … Now sing it again … In Ajoy Chakrabarty's voice.' And I would start singing all over again … in 'my voice'.

I am thankful to God that my father was so strict about my individuality. He gave me my sense of self-respect. He made me realise that my natural voice was a much better mirror of Ustad Bade Ghulam Ali Khan Saheb's *gayaki* than my trying to sing like my Ustadji.

I have tried to inculcate this value in all my students. Time and again I remind them that if they really want to be good singers then they must learn to listen to their voices.

Pandit Ajoy Chakrabarty's gurus nourished his thirst for *jnan* (knowledge). They cultivated his sense of inquisitiveness. They sowed the seeds of self-criticism in him. They ingrained in him the *samarthya* (capability) to explore further and unravel the true meaning of music. They proved to him that love has to be the foundation of a guru-*shishya* relationship. They taught him that

Young Ajoy Chakrabarty, full of hopes and aspirations

a good guru does not always lead the way. They taught him by example that a good guru shows the way and inspires a student to walk the path under the guru's guiding presence.

A true guru-*shishya* relationship pervades time and space. A guru never leaves his student even after moving on from the physical world because the guru is not a person but an idea, a concept, a power source—an all-pervading thought.

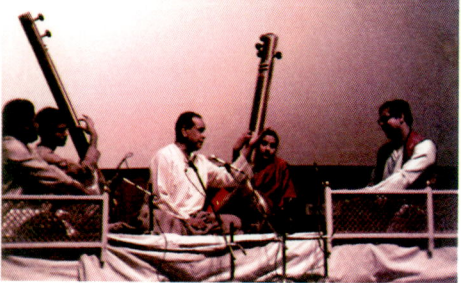

Ajoy Chakrabarty performs with Pandit Bhimsen Joshi at Netaji Indoor Stadium, Kolkata

Musical excellence is un-certifiable. No certificate can capture it. The same is true about a guru. A good student must work with unconditional *samarpan* (surrender) to the guru. A great guru must love his student unconditionally and give without demanding anything in return.

When I look back, I realise that my gurus were extensions of the almighty himself who held my hand lovingly and took me out from darkness to put me on the path of enlightened music.

In 1984, the Government of India awarded Guru Jnan Prakash Ghosh with the Padma Bhushan. It was a moment of great pride and joy for Ajoy Chakrabarty and his other disciples. Ajoy revelled in his guru's recognition. In a year's time, however, his guru had reason to cheer for his disciple too. The rhythmic cycle of Ajoy Chakrabarty's hard work and dedication over the years came

to rest on the *sam* or foundational beat of huge recognition. ITC Sangeet Research Academy's first scholar, Ajoy Chakrabarty, was appointed as a guru at ITC Sangeet Research Academy in 1985.

When news reached his Shyamnagar home, his father Ajit Chakrabarty's hands folded in an involuntary gesture of gratitude. Touching them to his forehead, his eyes closed in reverence, his lips parted and the words came out, 'Jai Guru! Jai Ma!' The prophecy of his spiritual guru, Sri Premananda Tirthaswami Maharaj came back to him. Ajit Chakrabarty opened his eyes to see the joy on the faces of Ajoy's *Bado Ma* and *Chhoto Ma*. He went inside and taking down his long-shirt from the hook on the wall, he put it on, picked up his umbrella, came out, and said to his wives, 'I am going to offer puja at the Kali temple. I will get some fish too.'

Ajoy Chakrabarty's elevation to the status of a guru also brought with it his appointment to the Experts Committee of the ITC Sangeet Research Academy. Selection to the Experts Committee was humbling and somewhat embarrassing too, because as an 'expert' Ajoy Chakrabarty was expected to share the platform with his mentor Guru Jnan Prakash Ghosh, who was also on the same committee along with stalwarts like Shri Raichand Boral, Pandit V.G. Jog, Pandit D.T. Joshi, Pandit A. Kanan,

Ajoy Chakrabarty's honoured Guruji Gnan Prakash Ghosh

Vidushi Malavika Kanan and Ustad Yunus Khan, besides Pandit Vijay Kichlu.

The committee met in traditional style. We sat on the floor. There were side pillows to lean on. I could never get myself to relax and lean on one of them in front of the stalwarts present in the room, as it would show disrespect. The fact that I was sitting amongst them was humbling enough at that age. Guruji, however, was very happy to see me on the Experts Committee. When I touched his feet before the first meeting of the committee and looked into his eyes I saw a blissful smile on his face. He seemed to have heard what I was trying to say … No matter how high I rise, my place will always be at the feet of my gurus!

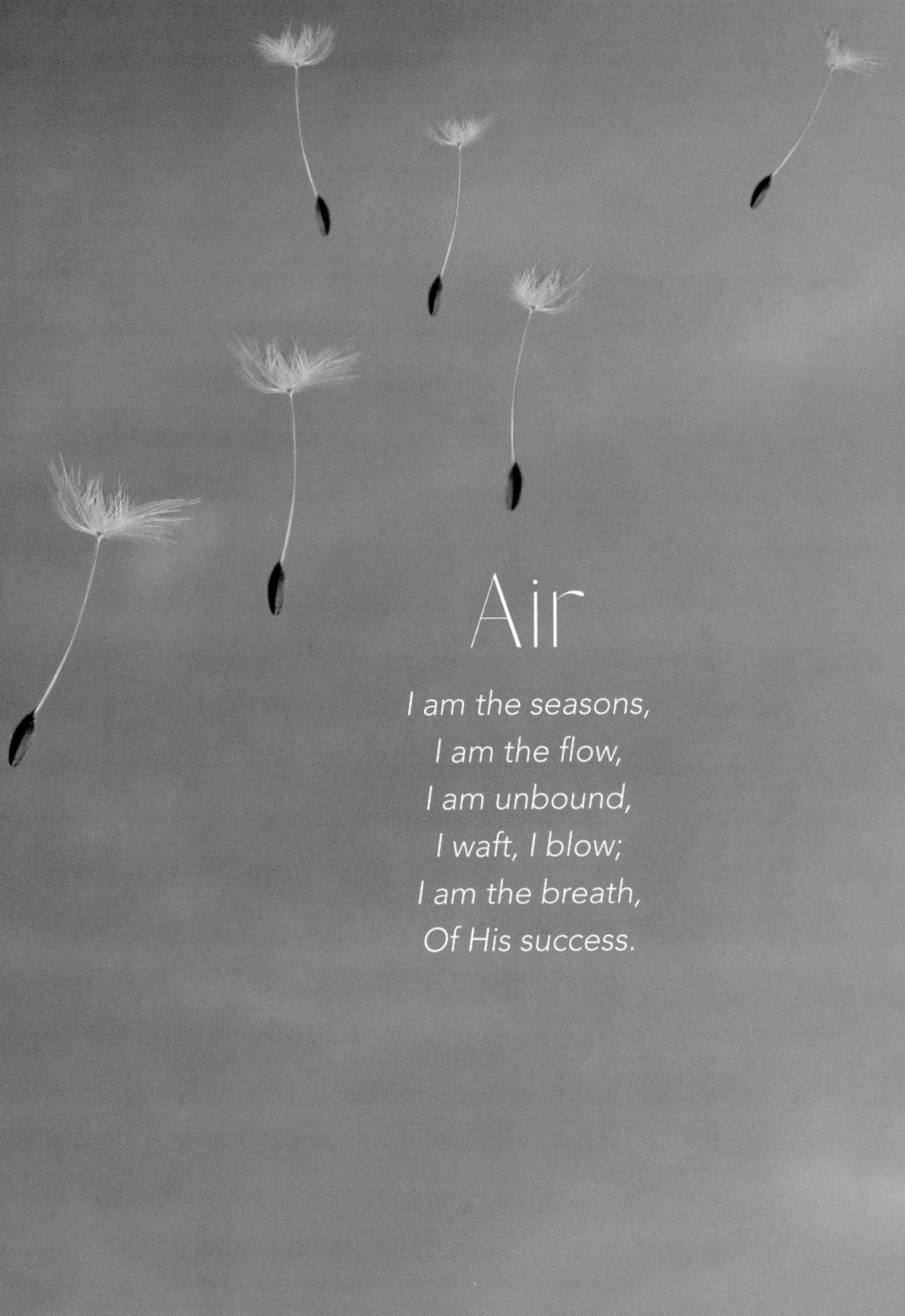

Air

I am the seasons,
I am the flow,
I am unbound,
I waft, I blow;
I am the breath,
Of His success.

sa

Ajoy Chakrabarty with Pandit V.G. Jog on violin, Arun Bhaduri on harmonium and Ananda Gopal Bandopadhyay on tabla, at ITC Sangeet Sammelan, 1983

From 1985 onwards, Ajoy Chakrabarty started performing regularly for ITC Sangeet Research Academy. Far from his home in Bengal a string of *sangeet sammelans* and concerts had started making Ajoy Chakrabarty a sought-after artiste in music-loving towns and cities like Varanasi, Lucknow, Pune, Trivandrum, Kottayam, Chennai, Jaipur, Ahmedabad, Sagar, Datia, Sholapur, Bijapur, Bidar, Gulbarga, Nagpur, Akola, Gondia and innumerable other cities and towns in the heartland of India.

My first international tour was to the USA in 1983, as an ITC Sangeet Research Academy scholar. It was also my first airplane journey. The ITC Sangeet Research Academy's journeys were like family outings. They were great

Ajoy Chakrabarty in concert with Pandit Hiru Ganguly

learning experiences too, because I got the opportunity to learn so much from the numerous interactions that we had on these trips. Pandit V.G. Jog, Pandit Shiv Kumar Sharma, Pandit Hari Prasad Chaurasia, Ustad Zakir Hussain, Pandit Vijay Kichlu ... some very impassioned classical artistes got to spend time together and interact amongst themselves. Always a keen learner ready to learn from everyone, I soaked in all the knowledge I could.

In 1984, I also had the unique privilege to be the first Indian classical vocalist to perform in Pakistan. It was a daunting proposition. I was there for 10 days. There was a concert or a *baithak* every evening and it went on till the early hours of the morning. The audience included connoisseurs

Ajoy Chakrabarty performs at Victoria Memorial Hall, Kolkata, at ITC Sangeet Sammelan, in December 2015

and practitioners of music who were well versed in the *gayaki* of the Patiala gharana. There were stalwarts who had known Ustad Bade Ghulam Ali Khan Saheb and even performed with him. The great Urdu poet Faiz Ahmad Faiz was in the audience every evening. Ghulam Ali bhai used to be there. I will never forget the love and admiration that was showered on me. I came back with many blessings and the realisation that music can speak the language of love and harmony like no other art can.

In 1985–86, the Festival of India in the US was a huge event. I got an opportunity to perform lecture-demonstrations in many cities in the United States as part of the festival circuit. Too much was

happening and it was happening very fast. None of it would have happened when it did, if ITC Sangeet Research Academy had not happened to me.

After 1985, Pandit Vijay Kichlu started involving Ajoy Chakrabarty in the management of ITC Sangeet Research Academy and he became more and more involved in the running of the institution that had given him so much.

The ITC Sangeet Research Academy gave me my persona. It gave me my understanding of what I stood for and helped me in understanding what made me the Ajoy Chakrabarty that

Ajoy Chakrabarty performs with Kumar Bose (on tabla) at ITC Sangeet Sammelan, in December 2015

I was and what could make me the Ajoy Chakrabarty that I really should be. In short, the ITC Sangeet Research Academy has been my altar of self-realisation. It will therefore always remain a place of worship for me.

ITC Sangeet Research Academy transformed scholar Ajoy Chakrabarty into Guru Ajoy Chakrabarty.

In putting him in the centre of the finest pool of talent that existed in the world of Hindustani classical music, the ITC Sangeet Research Academy taught Ajoy to discern between the good and the not-so-good in all aspects of music. It also went on to turn the *saadhak* (practitioner) of the swara into a *sevak* (servant) of the *swara*.

The ITC Sangeet Research Academy also helped in shaping my dream of creating a wholesome music learning institution for little children. It is the soil from which the flower of Shrutinandan bloomed. I regard Pandit Vijay Kichlu as one of my gurus. His zeal and passion in creating the ITC Sangeet Research Academy became an ideal for me. In Kichlu Saheb, I found an inspiration that later gave me the confidence to create Shrutinandan.

When ITC Sangeet Research Academy's scholar Ajoy Chakrabarty became ITC

Ajoy Chakrabarty felicitated by Pandit Mallikarjun Mansur in the presence of brother Sanjay Chakrabarty and Timir Roy Chowdhury

Sangeet Research Academy's Guru Ajoy Chakrabarty many things changed. The recognition gave him a sense of fulfilment and at the same time it put him centre-stage in the world of classical music that was eagerly looking forward to celebrating the rise of new stars. The horizon was already sparkling with names of vocalists like Pandit Bhimsen Joshi, Vidushi Kishori Amonkar, Pandit Jasraj, Pandit C.R. Vyas and more senior stars like Pandit Mallikarjun Mansur and Pandit Kumar Gandharva in the late 1970s and early 1980s. Ajoy Chakrabarty had no misgivings about his stature. He knew this was just another beginning.

The road was long and tough. For the next 10 years or so Ajoy Chakrabarty performed prolifically across the country. During these years he also recorded his music extensively.

re

As early as 1979 Ajoy had captured the fancy of Bengal with his rendition of Guru Jnan Prakash Ghosh's raga-based Bangla compositions like '*Kaare ba shonai*'. This was followed by albums like *Tomari Gaahi Joy* (I Sing Your Glory), *Sharad Anjali* (Autumnal Offering) and *Raager Bahare* (In the Spring of Ragas) in the first part of the 1980s. He endeared himself to audiences with his own style of rendering classics like Begum Akhtar's '*Piya bholo abhimaan*' (written and scored by Guru Jnan Prakash Ghosh). '*Bhorer shishir hoye*' from the 1987 Bangla album *Surer Surabhi* (The Fragrance of *Swaras*) remains a top request in concerts even today. When he sang '*Doorey aaro doore*' (Far, Further) in 1989 his audiences wanted Ajoy Chakrabarty's music to come closer and closer. He had redefined Bengal's love for light classical songs all over again. He gave new reach and expression to the lyrics of songwriters like Jatileshwar Mukherjee, Shyamal Gupta, Pulak Bandopadhyaya, Gauri

Ajoy Chakrabarty felicitates eminent playback singer Manna Dey at Shrutinandan in 2012

Ajoy Chakrabarty with (from left) Nachiketa, Rashid Khan, Banasree Sengupta, Firoza Begum, Dwijen Mukhopadhyay, West Bengal Chief Minister Mamata Banerjee, Sandhya Mukhopadhyay, Nirmala Mishra, Girija Devi, Arati Mukhopadhyay and Amar Pal at the Banga Bibhushan Award celebration

Prasanna Majumdar, Amalendu Bikash Kar Chowdhury, Jayanta Sarkar and his younger brother Sanjay Chakrabarty.

> Growing up in a *swara*-filled family, my younger brother Sanjay and I had shared a musical bonding since childhood. He was an important part of my growing up years. There is so much that we did together including going to school. A composer, a vocalist, a sitarist, a writer and a music-researcher with deep interest in studying the healing powers of music, Sanjay was always multi-talented and had a multi-spectral interest in music and music literature. Some of my most memorable concerts and recordings have Sanjay playing the harmonium with me. Some of my most memorable Bangla songs were written and composed by Sanjay.

What made Ajoy Chakrabarty's Bangla songs very special was that these songs that were steeped in different ragas were coming from a pure classical vocalist, who was being hailed as a maestro in the making by connoisseurs of Hindustani classical music across the world.

His soul-stirring raga renditions were equally sought after too. Albums of ragas were making waves in music shops in India and abroad. Amongst other releases came EMI Pakistan's landmark release of the five-album pack, *Ajoy*

Chakrabarty: Live in Pakistan, loaded with Pandit Ajoy Chakrabarty's fabulous rendition of *Hamir, Kedar, Malkauns, Bageshwari* and *Lalit* amongst other ragas. It was a heady combination that spoke volumes about the repertoire that Pandit Ajoy Chakrabarty had built at the young age of 32.

HMV India did an almost back-to-back release of the rarely heard Raga *Aheer-Lalit* and *Adana* topping it up with the heart-touching Misra Maand *dadra* 'Sanwariya anokhi tori chaturaayi'. The album had an introduction by the great film maker Satyajit Ray.

With the release of the Bangla feature film *Chhandaneer* in 1989, Ajoy Chakrabarty who had become a household name in Bengal, garnered nationwide attention by winning the National Award for the Best Male Playback Singer 'for bringing rare depth of emotion, adorned by his command on the classical idiom' to the songs of the film. The citation encapsulated what audiences had been saying about Pandit Ajoy Chakrabarty all along. It was big news. Only three other Bengali singers had won the award before him for a Bangla film—the two playback legends Shri Manna Dey (for *Nishi Padma*) and Shri Hemanta Kumar (for *Nimantran* and *Lalan Fakir*) and popular Nazrul Geeti singer Shri Anup Ghoshal (for Satyajit Ray's *Hirak Rajar Deshe*).

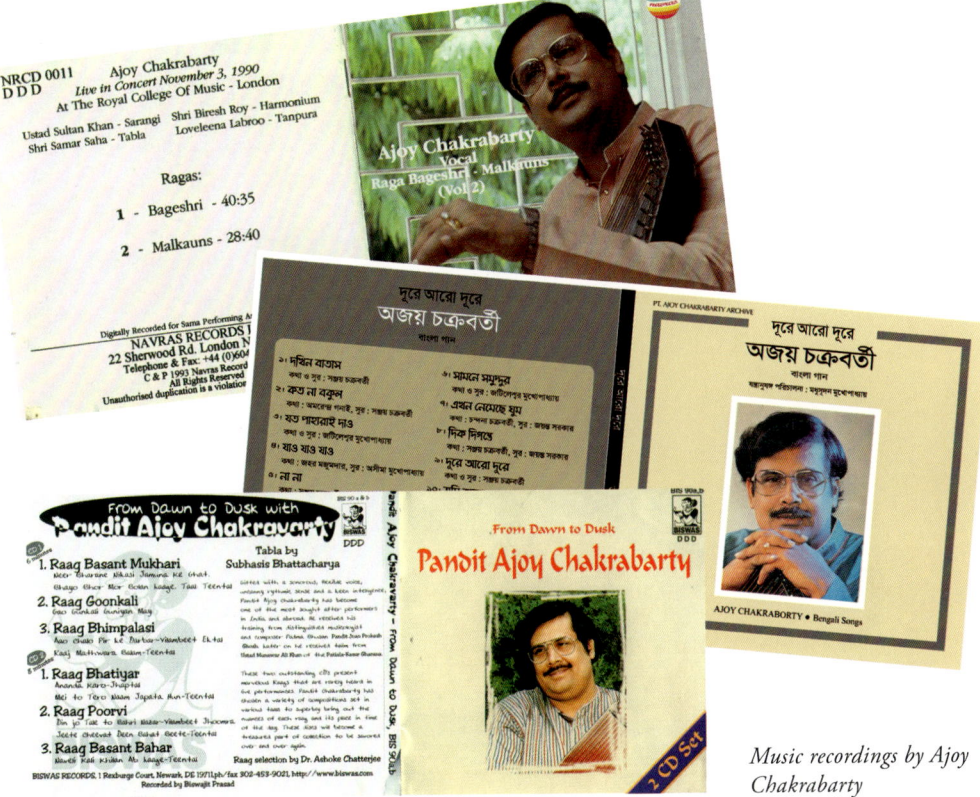

Music recordings by Ajoy Chakrabarty

Concert after concert followed in the second half of the 1980s and the first half of the 1990s in far-flung places in India and abroad, including a performance at the Royal College of Music in London in 1990.

I am not very good at remembering dates. In fact, I am not good at all. The Royal College of London concert was on 3 November 1990. I remember it because it is mentioned in the album that Navras Records, London released after some time. I sang *Malkauns*, *Behag*, and *Bageshwari*. Of course, in those days and sometimes even now,

I was not allowed to get up without singing Ustad Bade Ghulam Ali Khan Saheb's immortal '*Hari om tatsat*' or '*Aye na baalam*'. I think Ustad Sultan Khan who was on the sarangi and my friend Pandit Samar Saha who was on the tabla spurred me on to sing both of them that evening.

Guruji (Guru Jnan Prakash Ghosh) always said, 'When a guest comes to your house do not offer him food that has been lying in the refrigerator. Cook afresh and serve whatever you can. It need not be an elaborate affair. The dish can be simple but not what has been served before. Avoid

Ustad Zakir Hussain performs with a picture of Ajoy Chakrabarty in the background

repeating the items that you offer to your audience. Avoid repeating ragas and compositions. Try to sing something new, create something new or experiment with something new every day.' Sometimes repetition is unavoidable but as a rule I have tried to live up to his advice. But there are some compositions that have become much bigger in stature than their composers—bigger than even Ustad Bade Ghulam Ali Khan Saheb. 'Aye na baalam', 'Yaad piya ki aaye' and 'Hari om tatsat' belong to this category.

When there was more than a fair presence of Bengalis in the audience there was always a demand for one of my Bangla raga-based songs, or a Nazrul Geeti or a Shyama Sangeet but I made it a rule to avoid them in a pure classical concert. Of course, on some very rare occasions I had to relax my rule.

On the 1990 Europe tour, amongst other places, I also sang in Florence in Italy. I remember it for two reasons— one, because there was no stage and two, because Ustad Zakir Hussain, who was a world superstar by all measures accompanied me on the tabla and Kichlu Saheb on the tanpura. People like them are giants not just on the scale of contribution to music but also on the scale of human goodness and humility. Zakir Bhai, who is like an elder brother to me, has also played tanpura with my singing. I, on my part, have also enjoyed accompanying him on the tanpura and the harmonium on some occasions. Given a chance, I think I would do that with great joy even today.

A landmark album tilted *Thumri: The Music of Love*, which includes some *dadra*s was released in the same year with Ustad Zakir Hussain playing the tabla. The album, which includes the lilting *Misra Kafi thumri* 'Kaun jatan se preet nibhaaun' and the spritely *Mishra Khamaj thumri* 'Damini damke jiara mora larje' remains very close to Pandit Ajoy Chakrabarty's heart, because his Guru Pandit Jnan Prakash Ghosh decided to wield the harmonium. At the time of the recording he was almost 80 years old. His fingers, however, still covered the three octaves of the harmonium with youthful delight.

Concerts like the one at Queen Elizabeth Hall, London, in 1993 or the one in Philadelphia in 1994 that were a part of extensive tours of Europe, USA and Canada reached fans in the form of eagerly awaited album releases. The first featured a classic rendition of *Megh* and *Bhoopali* ragas and the latter, *Kedar*. Around the same time Pandit Ajoy Chakrabarty did a landmark recording of Raga *Khammaj* in all its forms in Broadway, New York. Of course, in all

Ajoy Chakrabarty and Rashid Khan in a concert

these years, his Bangla releases had been winning laurels too.

I was now performing full-fledged. Each concert was a moment of introspection. In the early 1990s, when I was around 40, I had the first feeling of having evolved into a good artiste. The years had raced by. I was now popular. Now I really had confidence. Maharashtra, which is always a difficult circuit to impress, had accepted me with great love and lot of expectations. I think I lived up to them. Mumbai had embraced me. Goa became a weekly affair. Sundays meant Goa. Having referred to senior musicians as Pandit and Ustad, it initially sounded a bit strange when 'Pandit' started being prefixed to my name in some of the promotions and announcements. I guess with time one gets to accept the title with graciousness. With time, I too accepted it with humility and gratitude.

'Pandit Ajoy Chakrabarty' … I was still not used to it, but someone must have been really smiling on hearing that prefix in Shyamnagar. I wish I could have seen the smile on my father's face, because whenever I stood in front of my father or my mothers, I was always their little son Ajoy. Some relationships never change. They should not.

ga

Ludwig Van Beethoven once said, 'To play a wrong note is insignificant but to play without passion is inexcusable.' Pandit Ajoy Chakrabarty was playing to his passion. To people who could not understand his passion, it seemed that he was playing wrong notes—not literally, but on the harmonium of life.

By 1994 Pandit Ajoy Chakrabarty released about 32 long playing records of *khayals*, *thumri-dadra*, bhajans and a variety of Bangla raga-based songs. From time to time, there was a film hit too. 'Where was Pandit Ajoy Chakrabarty going? How can a classical vocalist indulge in so many forms of music? Shouldn't *raga sangeet* be about being focused on *raga sangeet* only? He is diluting the focus.' Through the 1990s, and later too, Pandit Ajoy Chakrabarty's immense versatility and his unrestricted embrace

Ajoy Chakrabarty with Soumitra Chatterjee at Shrutinandan, 2018. In the background a photograph of Panditji singing for the film Shakha Proshakha *in the presence of Oscar winning director Satyajit Ray and Smt. Bijoya Ray*

of the musical note as God in one of his most beautiful forms, sparked many amusing discussions amongst purists, as well as general listeners.

People love a debate. Bengalis have formalised this to perfection by institutionalising what is called an '*adda*', a unique leisure activity that provides staple intellectual diet for small gatherings of Bengalis of all ages almost every evening. Wherever these gatherings included classical music lovers, they also discussed and debated Ajoy Chakrabarty's new serious interest in Carnatic music.

I performed with Vidwan Balamurali Krishnaji for the first time in the early 1980s in Calcutta. He was about 23 years older than me and one of the senior most star-musicians of the country. It was his graciousness that he gave his consent to do a *jugalbandi* with someone as junior as I was.

There was a big audience that day in the indoor stadium in Calcutta—running into many thousands. The size of the audience did not unnerve me but the fact that I had to sing with a stalwart like Balamuraliji did. The concert went off very well, but I realised that it may not go off well every time.

Ajoy Chakrabarty in concert with Dr M. Balamuralikrishna at Rabindra Sadan, Kolkata, 2012

I have heard many such experiments going absolutely off-track and ending in chaos. I needed to understand the dynamics of Carnatic music. I decided to learn Carnatic music more seriously.

From *kriti*s and *ragam, tanam, pallavi* to the *tani avartanam*, I explored the world of Carnatic raga music with Balamuraliji as my guru. It was a fascinating experience. He took me beyond just the shared heritage of Hindustani and Carnatic ragas and their commonalities and differences. He took me into the beauty of the heritage and its *sahitya* too. I must add that in all these concerts it was

Guru Balamuraliji who decided what was to be presented. So, I had to learn a lot. It helped that Balamuraliji himself was not tied down to the rigidity of old traditions. He did not insist on my singing the *gamaka*s exactly the way he did.

We performed together in Carnegie Hall in New York in 1985 during the Festival of India in the USA. Many other stalwarts performed too. The next day there was a huge report in the New York Times on the performance. A photo of our *jugalbandi* dominated the page. The others, who were all senior to me and really famous, teased

Ajoy Chakrabarty with Dr M. Balamuralikrishna and Srikanta Acharya at Science City Auditorium, Kolkata, 2015

A selection of album covers and press clippings of Pandit Ajoy Chakrabarty

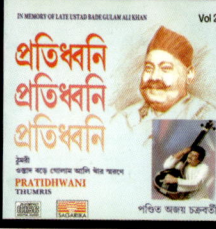

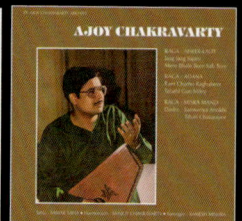

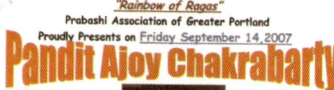

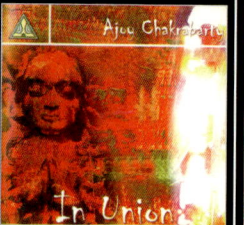
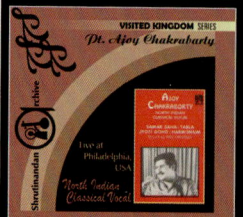

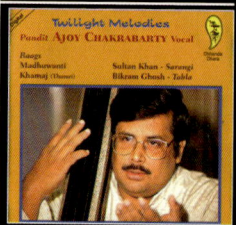

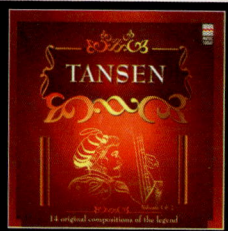
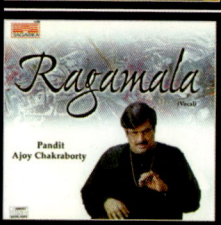
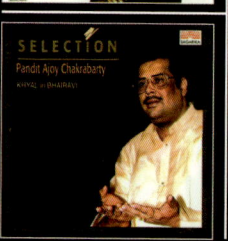

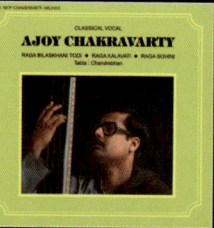
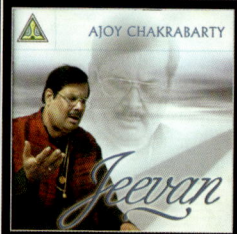

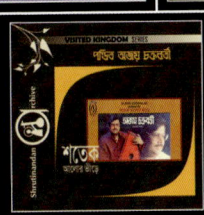

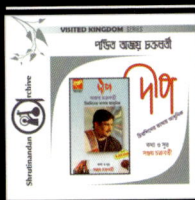

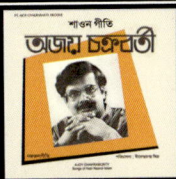

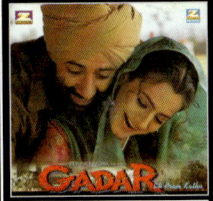

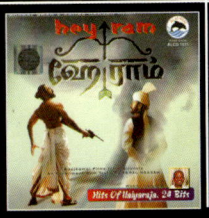

Ajoy Chakrabarty at Patiala Heritage Festival, 2018

me for garnering all the attention by performing with Balamuraliji but it was all in jest. They had tremendous love for me.

I recorded ragas *Abhogi* and *Hamsadhwani* for Music Today's Master's Choice (Series 3) with my guru Balamuraliji's blessings. Even to this day, I enjoy singing Muthuswami Dikshitar's epic *'Vatapi ganapatim bhajeham'* in my concerts. I miss him. Balamuraliji was a great artiste and a great supporter of Shrutinandan. He was also the President of Shrutinandan Trust for some years. He visited Shrutinandan and shared valuable insights with the students and teachers. He referred to me as his son.

Pandit Ajoy Chakrabarty had not been taught to differentiate one kind of music from another either by his parents or by his gurus. The spectrum that Pandit Ajoy Chakrabarty had inherited stretched like a hundred rainbows in an endless sky. Rainbows that included the subtle violet of Bade Ghulam Ali Khan Saheb's *'Jogan ban jaaun'* danced upon by Madhubala in the film Mughal-e-Azam, the blue mood of a mesmeric *'Kaa karun sajani aaye na baalam'*, the sunshine yellow of a divine *'Hari om tatsat'*, the sunset orange of the lady love crying *'Ab tohe jaane nain doongi'*, the blood red offering of a Kali kirtan, and innumerable *bandishes* in almost every raga.

Imagine caging the sky. Imagine holding back the rainbow. Everyone cannot visualise the larger picture. This may not be seen through the keyhole of locked minds.

ma

Ustad Munawar Ali Khan Saheb had passed away in 1989. He was just 59 years old and at the peak of his career at that time. In the untimely passing away of his ustad, Pandit Ajoy Chakrabarty lost a selfless *rahnuma* (guide).

Ustadji was full of love. The humaneness and generosity of his father coursed in his blood too. I learnt from him for many years; he never took any money from me. I rarely left his home without tasting the biryani, because he never let me leave without having it. It is also true that I have never had such biryani ever again. Maybe it was so special because it was spiced with affection. In having it—before I shifted to ITC-SRA in Kolkata—I sometimes missed the last train to Shyamnagar. Missing the train meant sleeping the night on the platform. I would catch the first train in the morning, have a bath at home and come back for the next instalment of both—Ustadji's invaluable teaching and Ammi's incomparable biryani. That day, when my father scolded me about my habits and behaviour being so different from Ustadji's, I should have told him that I did have the privilege of having some of Ustadji's biryani.

Ustad Munawar Ali Khan

Ajoy Chakrabarty and Anindo Chatterjee pay their respects to Guru Jnan Prakash Ghosh

Pandit Jnan Prakash Ghosh, who with his deep insight had sent his disciple Pandit Ajoy Chakrabarty to Ustad Munawar Ali Khan to imbibe the Kasur-Patiala heritage, had also advanced in years. He touched the age of 80 the year Ustad Munawar Ali Khan passed away. Over the decades, Guru Jnan Prakash Ghosh's relationship with his beloved disciple had become a paternal bond. As he grew older he often told Pandit Ajoy Chakrabarty, 'Ajoy, you have to complete the tasks that I leave incomplete. Promise me that you will.'

When he said this—and he said it quite often—I told him, 'Guruji, you are going nowhere.' He would smile and say, 'Only a person's body of work stays.' On such occasions, I remembered his early advice, 'Draw a very long line that inspires others to draw a longer one.' I wanted to draw this line in his lifetime. Deep in my heart I knew what his dream was. I knew that Guruji was not talking of my winning worldwide acclaim with concerts. Many of his talented disciples were already doing that. Guruji dreamt of creating a music-loving, music-understanding, music-enriched generation of Indians. He wanted me to think in this direction.

Great dreams are dreams that are dreamt for the benefit of others, but

Shri Buddhadeb Bhattacharya felicitating Ajoy Chakrabarty, after he received the first Kumar Gandharva Samman from the Government of Madhya Pradesh in 1993

they become great only when someone makes them come true. Pandit Ajoy Chakrabarty had just about taken off in his career as a performer, so it was only prudent that he should continue focusing on his career as a vocalist. His guru's words however stayed with him. He kept thinking about them in the first quarter of the 1990s.

Around the same time, a proposal was taking shape in Bhopal, the capital of the central Indian state of Madhya Pradesh. One of the greatest classical vocalists of India, Pandit Kumar Gandharva, who was born in Belgaum in Karnataka, but had made Dewas in Madhya Pradesh his home, passed away on 12 January 1992.

In 1992–93 the Government of Madhya Pradesh instituted the Kumar Gandharva Samman, a national award for excellence in the field of Indian classical music to be given to one exceptional artiste in the age group of 25 to 45 years. A high-profile committee consisting of leading musicians and experts scanned the nation to choose the first awardee and selected Pandit Ajoy Chakrabarty as the first recipient of the iconic award. It was another threshold moment in a life full of struggle and toil. The Kumar Gandharva Samman included a citation and a cash award of Rs 51,000. The young maestro in the making put aside the money received in a bank. He wanted time to reflect on his journey. He wanted to think.

Coming close on the heels of the National Award for Best Male Playback Singer, the acclaim for the Kumar Gandharva Samman echoed loudly in Pandit Ajoy Chakrabarty's home state, West Bengal. The Government of West Bengal too decided to felicitate the young maestro.

> It was a humbling moment in my life when Shri Buddhadeb Bhattacharya, who was then the Minister for Information and Cultural Affairs in West Bengal and later became the Chief Minister of the state decided to felicitate me publicly in Kolkata.
>
> The state government also decided to gift me a residential apartment in Kolkata as a reward for winning the Kumar Gandharva Samman. I felt honoured but I refused the offer with an apology. Buddhadeb Babu was surprised and asked why I was refusing the offer of a residential apartment. I explained that I did not need a flat to stay. I was happy in my Aldeen home in the ITC Sangeet Research Academy. And I had no intention of accepting a flat only to sell it off later at a profit.
>
> I then put aside my reluctance and managed to say, 'Give me a small piece of land instead, where I can one day fulfil someone's dream.'

'What do you want to do?' he asked.

I told him that I wanted to establish something that could enable me to be of service to the cause of Indian music. I was honest that I did not have a concrete plan as yet, but I hoped to put it together soon and that it was basically about creating a wondrous world of music where the musical spirit of little children could be nurtured.

They say that a path opens out to those who dare to walk the path. Shri Buddhadeb Bhattacharya agreed. The state government offered Pandit Ajoy Chakrabarty a huge piece of land in the Salt Lake institutional area on the outer edge of Kolkata. Pandit Ajoy Chakrabarty, however, preferred to accept a much smaller piece of land in Tollygunge, in the heart of town, close to his alma mater, ITC Sangeet Research Academy. He explained to the Chief Minister that the ITC Sangeet Research Academy was his home. It had given him everything and he did not want to leave it to fulfil his vision. It is on this land given by the Government of West Bengal on Golf Club Road in Tollygunge in Kolkata that Shrutinandan stands today.

Every story, however, has a prelude in which the story has its roots. In Shrutinandan's case this had to do with two little girls.

Shrutinandan—a school where musical dreams are perfected and realised

I was in the US with Chandana in 1987. Along with the whole country we had watched television coverage of the rescue of a little girl called 'Baby Jessica' who had fallen in a deep hole in the earth. Emotionally involved and concerned like millions of Americans who were glued to their television sets we also saw the larger story in this incident. The entire nation was standing up for one little child. We saw the importance given to the protection, health, upbringing and education of children in countries like the US.

Baby Jessica was rescued after three days. Like the rest of America, Pandit Ajoy Chakrabarty and Chandana also cheered with tears in their eyes when the little girl was brought out of the hole. On the flight back to India, Chandana told her husband, 'We should do something for children. Whatever we can with whatever we know and whatever we have.' Pandit Ajoy Chakrabarty turned to look at her. He did not say anything. He nodded and closed his eyes. A thought took birth. Years later this thought was given the name 'Shrutinandan.'

The other prelude to Shrutinandan has to do with the birth of a very beautiful little girl in Kolkata. God spent many hours tuning her very melodious voice before sending her to earth.

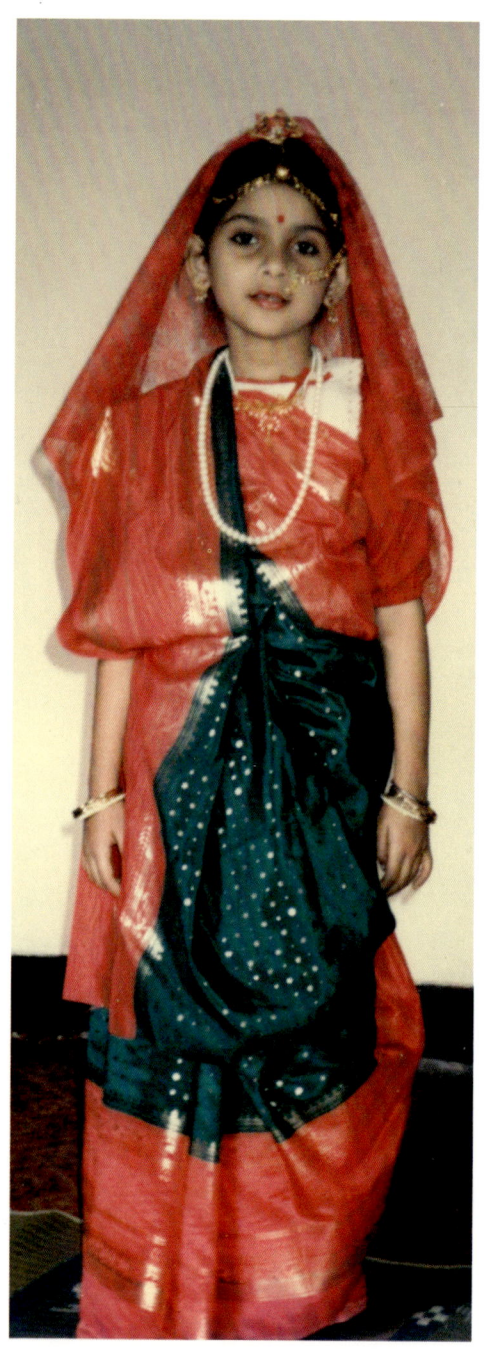

Young Kaushiki Chakrabarty

pa

Kaushiki Chakrabarty with her father at ITC Sangeet Research Academy

Pandit Ajoy Chakrabarty's marriage was the coming together of two musical inheritances—the inheritance that he received from his father and that which Chandana received from her mother, a disciple of *dhrupad* Guru Pandit Uday Bhattacharya (a descendent of the legendary Jadu Bhatt). Pandit Ajoy Chakrabarty had also learnt from him. These *samskaras* (impressions) must have been inherited by the beautiful little girl born to them on 24 October 1980. She looked like a doll and so they called her 'Putul' (Bangla for doll). Later she was ceremonially named Kaushiki.

Pandit Ajoy Chakrabarty's philosopher-friend Arindam Chakrabarti gave her the name Kaushiki. According to ancient Hindu beliefs, Kaushiki is a beauteous form of Shakti who was born out of the *kosha* (sheath) of the goddess. The

Young Kaushiki Chakrabarty

Vendantic text, *Taittriya Upanishad*, also refers to the *panch kosha* or the five sheaths in which our existence is enveloped.

The early years of our marriage were years of struggle. I lived in a much smaller accommodation in Aldeen, when Chandana was pregnant with Kaushiki. Those were times when Kolkata faced long power cuts. I remember coming back from day-long classes and fanning her with a hand-fan, all through the hours, when there was no power. She resisted, I insisted. I liked doing it and it never tired me. Kaushiki must have heard a lot of music in her mother's womb, because a lot of the fanning was accompanied by

remembering, recalling and repeating the lessons of the day—softly, of course.

Kaushiki was born in the lap of music. Music was the language most spoken, the subject most discussed, the activity most indulged in and musicians were the most frequent visitors to the Chakrabarty house. Growing up in this environment must have had a direct impact on her mind and intellect. And of course, her growing-up years were years in which Pandit Ajoy Chakrabarty practised 12 to 14 hours a day.

As a toddler Kaushiki often came and settled in my lap while I did my *riyaaz*. She would put her ear to my chest and listen to the vibrations of the notes

Young Kaushiki Chakrabarty with Arun Bhaduri, friends and family

very intently. When I shifted to singing notes that seemed to come from the belly she shifted her ears too. It was one of her favourite games.

Kaushiki struck up a lasting friendship with many ragas very early in her life. I am sure that she could identify the notes that make up an octave much before she learnt to speak.

There was music all around little Kaushiki. There was music and music-related talk of all kinds going into her ears. She was always amongst us. That apart, she must have been born with an ingrained, extraordinary flair for singing. Now I know that from about eight weeks onwards a baby starts responding well to sounds. With

Putul, it began surprisingly earlier. She was steeped in swaras. There was something very peaceful, very beautiful in the way she looked at us, when we held her in our arms as an infant. I am sure that it was a reflection of the kind of musical expression that was ingrained in her.

When Kaushiki was about 10 months old and was just about learning to walk, Pandit Ajoy Chakrabarty noted something extremely interesting. Like all musician parents, Pandit Ajoy and Chandana Chakrabarty were also extremely eager to know how melodious their child was. They noted something amazing. Every time they sang *Sa* (the first note of the octave, equivalent to

Ajoy Chakrabarty in concert with Shyamal Bose on tabla and Badal Pradhan on tanpura

the western *Do*) Kaushiki responded by saying *Sa*, but singing it in the fifth note of the same octave, that is, *Pa* (or *Sol*). This happened every time Pandit Ajoy Chakrabarty sang *Sa* in any scale. She kept singing *Pa* as her *Sa*! Kaushiki was born with a mastery over the crucial fifth note relationship. This is something that normally develops much later.

I shared my experience with Ustadji and he was amazed too. I requested him to come over one day, hear our daughter's voice and bless her. Ustadji came and for every *Sa* he sang, Kaushiki answered with a *Sa* in the fifth note. He smiled and said, 'Your daughter is

blessed by god. This is truly amazing for an infant. I think you should call her *Panchami* (fifth). May Allah grant her great success and happiness! Teach her well, Ajoy.'

This experience triggered the introspective thinker in Pandit Ajoy Chakrabarty. He had been taught to accept nothing without exploring it further. He started delving deeper into the amazing world of the octave and its constituent notes.

I started from the fact that *Sa* (*Do*) and *Pa* (*Sol*) have the same position in the octave. One is a reflection of the other

Ajoy Chakrabarty accompanying Kavita Krishnamurthy in concert

and *Sa, Re, Ga, Ma* or Do-Re-Mi-Fa is the exact transposition of *Pa, Dha, Ni, Sa* or Sol-La-Ti-Do. So, this means that there are actually four mool swaras (prime notes)—*Sa, Re, Ga* and *Ma*—*Pa, Dha, Ni* and *Sa* are its complimentary set of notes. So, it is not linear, but cyclic. *Sa, Re, Ga, Ma* meets *Pa, Dha, Ni, Sa* to create an unending cycle. Both the *Sa*s merge to create the axis.

Teevra Ma or F# is the bending point that bridges *Ma* and *Pa*. This bridging cannot be done by a *komal swara* or a flat note. Except *teevra Ma*, all the other half notes are flat notes. *Teevra Ma* emerges as the essential connector—the powerful convergence point. Centuries ago, Pythagoras had drawn the 'Circle of Fifths' for the western world. In Europe, solmisation or the practice of assigning syllables or names to the notes of the octave had grown out of the Indian use of the words *Sa, Re, Ga, Ma, Pa, Dha, Ni, Sa.*

My search was different. It had a lot to do with my child and subsequently with thousands of other children. My little daughter must have wondered why she had made me so thoughtful. When she grew up I told her that she was, and still remains, one of my gurus. Quite unintentionally, she had shown the light; she had shown the path.

dha

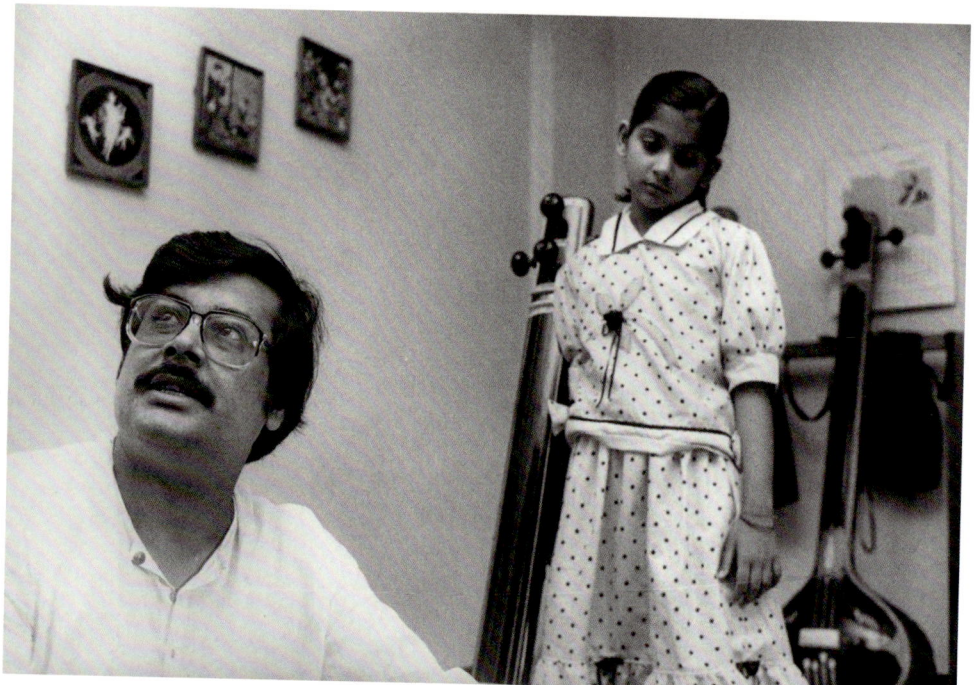

Young Kaushiki with Ajoy Chakrabarty

The path indicated by 'the Kaushiki experience' was virtually forbidden for a busy, practising, performing classical vocalist to whom the world had just started opening its warm embrace of adulation. But some paths have a way of calling out. If it is your call—the one embedded in your heart by the Almighty ages ago—then try as much as you can, you will not be able to shut it out. It will keep calling. You have the option of ignoring it and listening to the cravings of the mind but then, you will always remain unfulfilled, incomplete and ill-at-ease with all your achievements. These were Pandit Ajoy Chakrabarty's 84-hour practice-chakra years. The call kept echoing year after year. He did not shut it out. He did not want to.

Meanwhile, Kaushiki kept growing. Her music education started at home. Her mother Chandana was her first guru. She handed Kaushiki the joys of the *sargam*.

Pandit Ajoy Chakrabarty oversaw her progress very keenly. Concert after concert in India and abroad kept Pandit Ajoy Chakrabarty flying in and out of home. So, every moment that he could spend with Kaushiki became very special, very instructive and very constructive for both of them. Kaushiki's mother became the anchor of Kaushiki's music education. By the age of three Kaushiki could identify notes with instinctive sharpness.

Personal joys often bear the brunt of the pursuit of creative passion and excellence. Behind the applause that an artiste gets on stage are hidden many sacrifices and struggles in fulfilling personal and familial responsibilities. With a career that was moving at breakneck speed in the 1980s, I missed ensuring Kaushiki's timely admission to school. She was six when she joined school directly in the third standard. It needed the recommendation of none other than the great film maker and writer Shri Satyajit Ray, who was extremely fond of my singing.

One day Pandit Vijay Kichlu asked how Kaushiki's music education was progressing. When Pandit Ajoy Chakrabarty told him that it was going on at home, the short discussion that followed ended with the command, 'Ajoy, she has to learn formally, even if it has to be from you. The best thing for her would be to join the ITC Sangeet Research Academy as a scholar under you!'

History was repeating itself. Pandit Vijay Kichlu was once again playing the role of the all-important note of convergence— the 'teevra Ma' or F#— in Pandit Ajoy Chakrabarty's life.

I agreed with Kichlu Saheb but there was a problem. How could I become Kaushiki's guru without my guru's permission? I approached him with folded hands. He not only agreed to teach Kaushiki but also instructed me to prepare for the ganda bandhan ceremony, which he said he would perform in our house in Aldeen complex. I knew that Guru Jnan Prakash Ghosh did not believe in the ganda bandhan ritual. Whenever he had agreed to do it, the ceremony had always taken place in his house. This time he had decided to make an exception. His humanism, and, in

Ajoy Chakrabarty with Sreemat Sadananda Brahmachary Maharaj and Guru Jnan Prakash Ghosh

particular, his love and concern for children, was evident in his decision to come himself, instead of asking the student to come to his house. It was a unique gesture. Kaushiki's *ganda bandhan* ceremony became a very memorable event. Stalwarts of ITC Sangeet Research Academy including Pandit Nivrittibua Sarnaik, Kichlu Saheb, Pandit Sunil Bose, Ustad Latafat Hussain Khan Saheb and many other senior artistes blessed Kaushiki.

Kaushiki learnt from Guru Jnan Prakash Ghosh for about one-and-a-half years. He taught her small *bandish*es and some other compositions which he specially created for her. In the summer of 1987, little Kaushiki along with her mother joined Pandit Ajoy Chakrabarty on his extensive tour of the United States. She was just seven years old. Her talent, however, was way beyond the normal age-to-expectation scale. Pandit Ajoy Chakrabarty performed in 31 concerts on the tour. Kaushiki shared the stage with him in each one of them. The world's eyes were upon her. She won many thousand hearts in the US with a *palta* here, a *taan* there or a melodious bhajan.

ni

In 1989 Guru Jnan Prakash Ghosh handed the responsibility of Kaushiki's teaching to Pandit Ajoy Chakrabarty and she became a scholar at the ITC Sangeet Research Academy. Kaushiki was less than nine years old then and remains one of the youngest scholars ever to have joined the Academy. In Kaushiki's becoming an ITC Sangeet Research Academy scholar, the biggest transformation was not in her life but in the life of Pandit Ajoy Chakrabarty. The father had become the guru.

Personally speaking, it was a huge change. My approach to music teaching was full of love but very exacting. There was no room for leniency. I had to keep aside the thought that the little girl in front of me was my daughter. Not that I could ever forget it. Deep down I knew that for many years Kaushiki will be my disciple first and my daughter later.

More than the recipient of a father's love in the traditional sense Kaushiki became the recipient of advice, encouragement, praise, criticism and

Ajoy Chakrabarty and young Kaushiki in New York

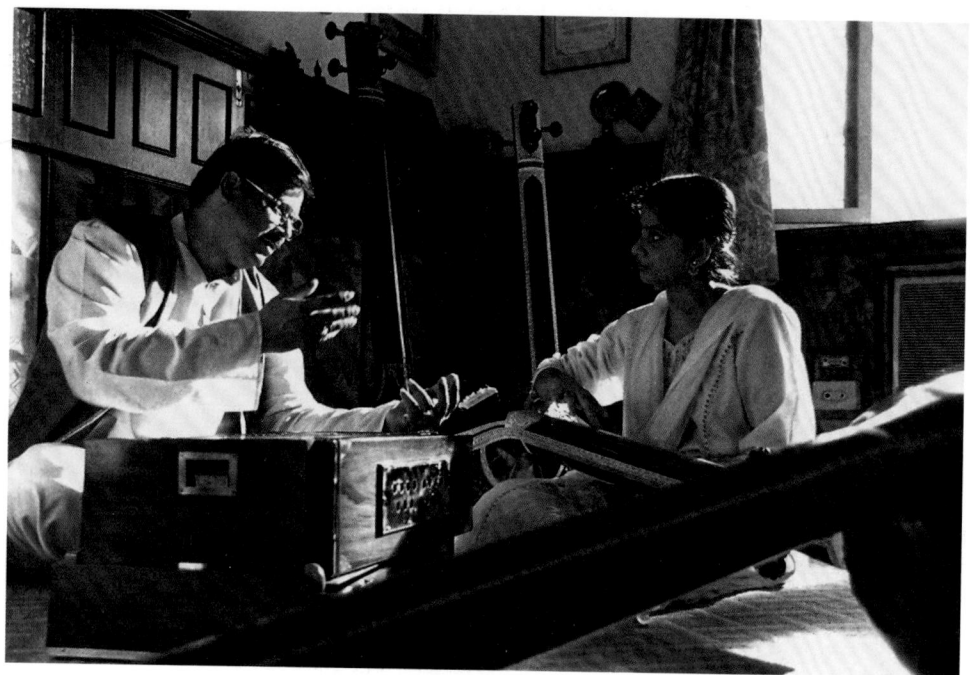

Kaushiki, the disciple, with her guru Ajoy Chakrabarty

constant training and evaluation. I missed my 'daughter' sometimes; she must have missed her 'father'. As I said earlier, the pursuit of passion calls for many a precious thing to be put into the sacrificial fire of honest efforts.

Pandit Ajoy Chakrabarty gave Kaushiki as much as he gave to any other student. There was no differentiation. There was a simple reason for this. In class, he only saw the student in Kaushiki and not his daughter. Kaushiki, who had amazing grasping powers, listened and learnt with her intellect. She never heard and replicated. She heard, thought, assimilated and rendered—all in the blink of an eye. She was a deep- and fast-thinking disciple. She internalised the knowledge that her guru imparted and she had immense faith in her guru. She followed Pandit Ajoy Chakrabarty's training to the last word.

One day Kaushiki was singing and I was sitting in the wings and watching her. We were in Delhi. She was still a child. Next to me was tabla maestro Ustad Alla Rakha Khan, Ustad Zakir Hussain's father. After some time, I felt his hand on my shoulder. I turned with folded hands. Almost in a whisper, he said, '*Isko bachaa kar rakhna, Ajoy. Mujhe is mein Zakir ke bachpan waali baat dikhti hai'* (Keep her protected, Ajoy. I see in her the talent that I saw in my son Zakir Hussain, when he was a child).

Due to her late start, Kaushiki waded through her early school education with difficulty and disinterest. Then a messiah called Professor Snehanshu Kumar Sarkar came into Pandit Ajoy Chakrabarty and Kaushiki's lives.

Some relationships are god-sent. They have nothing to do with birth or age. He was elder to me but he called himself my god-son. Chandana was 'Ma' to him. Professor Snehanshu Kumar Sarkar was full of *sneha* and *jnan* (love and wisdom). He struck an amazing chord with Kaushiki and kindled her interest in school education.

His way of teaching was very different. It was inspiring for me too. Here the reverse was happening. My daughter who was exceptional in music but totally ill-at-ease with her school curriculum was finding new interest in it. As a musician, I always transpose situations to the music scenario. I realised that this could also be done the other way around. Many children could be made to fall in love with music, without diluting its classicism, if it could be taught interestingly.

Professor Snehanshu Sarkar had sowed the seeds of Kaushiki's love for studies. His contribution in inspiring Kaushiki and in being a pillar of support for Pandit Ajoy Chakrabarty cannot be quantified.

By 1994, when Kaushiki was 13 years old and the very encouraging results of her music training had started coming through, Pandit Ajoy Chakrabarty also started seeing his first clear vision of an institution for teaching music to children in a revolutionary way.

The Shrutinandan system of teaching music evolved in the process of my teaching Kaushiki. Today Kaushiki is a celebrated artiste and I am confident that as long as she continues developing in the Shrutinandan system she is going to get better and better. She epitomises the success of the system. Learning is a never-ending process. I am still a learner. I am glad that I am totally comfortable being a learner, even after so many years. I shall be ever-grateful to Kaushiki for having been the perfect material for trying out my ideas and also for her having surrendered to her guru with total faith in him. Very few students do that. Her deep faith in me and the hard work she put in, helped shape my vision of Shrutinandan.

FACING PAGE

Top row, from left: *Ajoy and Chandana Chakrabarty with Kaushiki; A happy family, Ajoy and Chandana Chakrabarty with Kaushiki and Ananjan; Ajoy and Chandana Chakrabarty with his mother*

Middle row, from left: *Ajoy and Chandana Chakrabarty at their home; Ajoy Chakrabarty with his daughter and son in a concert; Ajoy Chakrabarty with his relatives*

Bottom row, from left: *Ajoy Chakrabarty conducting Durga Puja at home; Ajoy and Chandana Chakrabarty*

Top: *Chandana and Ajoy Chakrabarty with grandson Rishith, Kaushiki, son-in-law Parthasarathy Desikan and Ananjan (middle) Ajoy Chakrabarty enjoying a holiday with his family, (above) Ajoy Chakrabarty holds his grandson Rishith in the company of Chandana, Kaushiki and Ananjan*

Kaushiki and Ananjan Chakrabarty—the siblings share a deep musical bond

Space

I am limitless,
I am the quest,
I am freedom,
I am the glow,
I am my search,
I am His breath.

sa

There was a flurry of reactions when Pandit Ajoy Chakrabarty first broached the idea of creating an institution to teach music to children. If all these reactions could be turned into musical expressions and woven together into a *bandish* then they would create the most confused composition ever.

People who loved Pandit Ajoy Chakrabarty warned him not to step into the quicksand of emotions. There is a beautiful line in the 16th century Indian saint-poet Tulsidasji's *Ramacharitamanas*, 'Adhik sneh man bha sandeha' (too much love creates doubts in the mind). This is true. People who love you too much do not want to see you getting hurt or failing. Their love can become a source of weakness. 'Are you mad Ajoyji? You are a performing musician. Forget all this! Focus on your singing,' or 'The artiste in you will suffer! You cannot do both! You are putting your own career at stake,' or quite simply, 'You are just 42. This is not the age to do it. Do it later,' were some of the reactions to Ajoy Chakrabarty's decision to form an institution.

Pandit Ajoy Chakrabarty knew that there is nothing called 'later'. He had given up

this word some years ago. But neither was he in a rush to do anything. The confusion about what he was planning to do was around him, not in him. He still knew and he still believed in one of his favourite childhood songs:

'Maa aachhen aar aami aachhi, Bhabnaa ki aachhe aamaar'

[Mother (Ma Kali) is there and I am there. Why should I have any worry?]

Pandit Vijay Kichlu, however, was very worried. He loved Pandit Ajoy Chakrabarty like his son. He remembered that Sunday morning when he had first heard Pandit Ajoy Chakrabarty at Pandit A.T. Kanan's house. He remembered Pandit Ajoy Chakrabarty becoming the first scholar of ITC Sangeet Research Academy just 17 years ago. Having set up an institution, he knew its demands and warned Pandit Ajoy Chakrabarty, 'You risk spoiling your career, Ajoy. In my opinion, a practising musician should not run an institution. Don't do it now. I know what it takes to shape an institution and then run it well.'

I knew Kichlu Saheb was not wrong and I also knew that he only had my welfare and happiness at heart. Despite being

Ajoy Chakrabarty at an ITC Sangeet Research Academy forum with eminent musicians

one of the main forces behind the formation of ITC Sangeet Research Academy, he was one of the few who understood that I was not trying to walk away from ITC Sangeet Research Academy or using the experience gained to set up a parallel institution. Music education for small children was in any case a subject that was outside ITC Sangeet Research Academy's focal areas. In fact, I hoped to give ITC Sangeet Research Academy talented scholars one day. However, to do that

I did not want to leave ITC Sangeet Research Academy. I did not think that there was any need for that.

I told Kichlu Saheb, 'You have to be with me in spirit. You will have to light the inaugural lamp.' Kichlu Saheb knew that I was not one to step back. He said, '*Theek hai*' (All right then…) and then after a pause he smiled and said, '*Tum kar paogey*' (You will be able to do it).

Now I had to think, 'How?'

ITC Sangeet Research Academy honours Guru Pandit Ajoy Chakrabarty

Of course, there were other people too who pronounced judgment on the young maestro's decision. Intentions were questioned too. As far as Pandit Ajoy Chakrabarty was concerned he just reminded himself of Rabindranath Tagore's priceless lines: 'You cannot cross the sea by standing on the shore and staring at it.' People with honesty of purpose let their work speak. They let time speak. The young scholar who insisted on signing only a two-year bond with the ITC Sangeet Research Academy in 1980 remains an integral part of the spirit and soul of the academy even after four decades. Many have come and gone in these four decades.

There is a poem attributed to the 13th century Turkish Sufi saint, Maulana Jalaluddin Rumi in which he says:

Each one of us has been made
for a particular task!
The desire for that task has been
put in every heart!
Your path is yours alone!
Someone can walk it with you!
No one can walk it for you!

In 1995, Music Today's Gharana Series featured a double album by Pandit Ajoy Chakrabarty, acknowledging him as the leading interpreter of Patiala gharana's *gayaki*. Besides iconic *bandishes* in ragas *Deshkar, Multani* and *Hamir,* it

Ajoy Chakrabarty pays tribute to Ustad Bade Ghulam Ali Khan

features a fabulous rendering of Ustad Bade Ghulam Ali Khan Saheb's *Rageshri bandish 'Sab sukh diyo kartar'*.

Nothing would be more apt to describe Pandit Ajoy Chakrabarty's state of mind around 1995 than *'Sab sukh diyo kartar'* (Almighty! You have given me all the happiness I desired).

The *bandish* ends with Ustad Bade Ghulam Ali Khan imploring God to help fulfil the tasks he has on hand… *'Sabrang, morey kaaj sanwaaro.'* Ustad Bade Ghulam Ali Khan's Rageshri became Pandit Ajoy Chakrabarty's call to the divine. Ustad Bade Ghulam Ali Khan used to say, *'Riyaaz* (the formal

practice of music) is just another name for the five namaazes (Muslim prayers) and the eight poojas (Hindu prayers) of the day.' Pandit Ajoy Chakrabarty believed it to the last word! He prayed through his music.

One thing Pandit Ajoy Chakrabarty was sure of was that his dream needed money. The Bible says, 'Ask, and you shall receive!' Pandit Ajoy Chakrabarty did just that without really being very sure of the second part of the sentence— the receiving part—but that is exactly what happened. He asked for Rs 10 lakh (1 million) from Shri Sushim Mukul Dutta, then Chairman and Managing

Director of Hindustan Lever. Hindustan Lever Limited sanctioned a grant of Rs 1 crore (10 million) realising that what Pandit Ajoy Chakrabarty had asked for would help achieve nothing. What Pandit Ajoy Chakrabarty received was epic in proportion to what he had asked for. The fulfilment of his dream had now moved to the fast track.

Shrutinandan was inaugurated in July 1997, when Pandit Ajoy Chakrabarty was just 45 years old. As promised, Pandit Vijay Kichlu was there to light the inauguration lamp, but Pandit Ajoy Chakrabarty missed one man soulfully—the man who had given him the dream—Guru Pandit Jnan Prakash Ghosh. The great guru, great musician and great human being had passed away on 17 February 1997, just missing the rendezvous with his disciple's greatest day by a few months. Years later he remains the hub of Shrutinandan, as he is present in the form of his values and teachings in Shrutinandan's Jnan Prakash Ghosh Sanctum.

There was a lot of speculation as to what Ajoy Chakrabarty will do now. That which did not cross my thoughts at all was being attributed to my plans. Maybe many people had not really believed that I would actually go on to build an institution. Those who thought I would, were surprised how quickly it had come about. Frankly speaking, even I had not thought that things would happen so fast. The ITC Sangeet Research Academy also wondered how to handle this situation … what to do … how to respond. It had never envisaged that such a thing would happen.

I think the honesty of my approach made the difference. Honest efforts cannot be overlooked. Once the air cleared, most of the people realised that there was no clash of interests. At ITC Sangeet Research Academy the focus was on grooming advanced-level students to become high-quality performers. The journey of an advanced-level student starts in childhood and it is crucial to get high-quality music education as a child. I wanted to take a meaningful step towards bridging the institutional gap that existed. Shrutinandan's focus was on children younger than 12 years. It was not in any way going to compromise with my duties as a guru with ITC Sangeet Research Academy. I would not allow that. The ITC Sangeet Research Academy had nurtured me and I was not one to forsake my alma mater. Regardless of what anyone may think, I was my own uncompromising conscience keeper. And I remain so.

Pandit Ajoy Chakrabarty
at Shrutinandan

Young Kaushiki with Ajoy Chakrabarty in concert

Meanwhile, little Kaushiki Chakrabarty whose training had been foundational in the evolution of Shrutinandan's teaching system had started doing very well in academics too. Professor Snehanshu Kumar Sarkar and Patha Bhawan had combined to work wonders. Kaushiki went on to perform excellently in her class 10 and 12 board exams. Music education, including performances, went on too. A rank holder in Kolkata in her BA (Philosophy) exams, she finally went on to top the class in her master's in Philosophy from Jadhavpur University in Kolkata in 2002.

Kaushiki's academic results cemented Pandit Ajoy Chakrabarty's belief that formal education and music education of the highest kind—or for that matter art or talent-education of any kind and academics—can go on simultaneously. One does not have to be at the cost of the other.

Kaushiki got married to Pandit Ajoy Chakrabarty's student Parthasarathy Desikan in February 2004. The wedding was held with traditional fanfare in Pandit Ajoy Chakrabarty's parental home in Shyamnagar. Kaushiki and Parthasarathy have a son named Rishith who has inherited and imbibed the family's love for music.

Kaushiki Chakrabarty

re

The name 'Shrutinandan' was finalised after a lot of meditation on the concept. The 12 letters of the name are symbolic of the 12 notes (7 major notes, 4 flat notes, 1 sharp note) in the *saptak*. The first letter of the name S-H-R-U-T-I-N-A-N-D-A-N symbolises *Sa* (western *Do*) and the last symbolises *Ni* (western *Ti*). The name itself has two parts—Shruti and Nandan. *Shruti* means 'that which is heard' and *Nandan* is 'that which gives joy'.

For centuries, our music teaching has been very one-dimensional. It has always been based on 'individual training'. A teacher teaches what he or she has learnt in the same manner. God has blessed everyone with individuality. The focus should be on this 'individuality' and not on 'individual training' that is simply repetitive. Mindless repetition throttles the innate powers of a good disciple.

Every student is unique. Teaching art is about reaching out to a student's talent, nurturing his or her uniqueness and inspiring the student to give it wings. Whenever a student repeats a *taan* in a way that is not a mirror image of my *taan* but conforms with all that is required for correctness, I encourage the student. The results I get are very positive. I have stuck to this path and continue to get good results.

Great singers have not produced many great disciples. Wherever they have been able to it is because they did not ask their disciples to clone their music, their style, their voice.

A similarity will always be there between the guru and his disciple but it should never be at the cost of individual expression and excellence. If Ustad Zakir Hussain had been a replica of his father and guru Ustad Alla Rakha Khan Saheb then we would not have had a Zakir Hussain.

Kaushiki is said to be my finest student. She does not copy me in any way. When I hear that Kaushiki has gone ahead or will go ahead of Pandit Ajoy Chakrabarty it is something of great joy for me.

A student finds it difficult to develop uniqueness in learning from one guru only or being closeted in the walls of a gharana. Contrary to what some people believe, uniqueness actually comes from versatility. I had

At the launch of an album produced by Shrutinandan with Koel Mallick and Prasenjit

myself learnt all forms of music while growing up. They never came in each other's way.

The aim of the gharana system is not to create clones but the fact remains that in many cases it had become just that. Teaching art of any kind cannot be about creating clones. Gharanas lost their greatness wherever they took to following the 'copy your guru' path.

It is true that from time to time inspired individuals fired by a zeal to experiment and improvise added new creative patterns to the canvas of their gharana's traditions. Wherever this happened the gharana breathed a new lease of life.

Hear and repeat. Repeat and learn. Learn and reproduce. This decadent system of music education has its value in as much as it has helped to keep centuries-

old oral traditions and compositions alive. It does not however compare with the 'hear, see, and learn' method practiced at Shrutinandan—a method that does not take away anything from the importance of hearing and learning and yet gives a student of music the ability 'to see' a clear visible structure of *swaras* (notes) while singing or playing an instrument.

A *bandish*, a *thumri*, a *dadra* or a bhajan or any other song for that matter, is a sequence of musical sentences. Each musical sentence is a sequence of musical words. Each musical word is a set of musical letters. These letters are called *swaras* or notes. The Shrutinandan method is not about teaching how well one can repeat a musical sentence. It is about how well one can read, create and express a musical sentence.

My understanding of how one *swara* moves to another developed out of the unique music stenography exercise that my father made me do every day after I joined Guru Jnan Prakash Ghosh's class in 1969. It was mind boggling to write the lyrics, their notations and also to mark how

Left, from top to bottom: Ajoy Chakrabarty with Gobindo Rith (harmonium maker); with Binoy Biswas (tanpura maker); with Purbayan Chatterjee (sitarist); with Snehasis Majumdar (mandolin maestro)

Ajoy and Chandana Chakrabarty at Shrutinandan

the notes moved from one syllable to another in Rabindranath Tagore's songs while they were being played on the radio. Soon, I could see the jigsaw of notes like a grid in my mind —from letters (the 12 notes) to words (note combinations) to sentences and paragraphs. All this in a split second. I was not just hearing songs anymore, I had taken my first steps in being able to see them.

Many years later when I looked back on that exercise and its impact, I started thinking that if I could see musical notes in real time, then why couldn't others be taught to do so as well? This went on to become the basis of what can be called the 'Shrutinandan technique' of teaching and learning music.

The Shrutinandan system of music education has seven coordinates. It follows a scientific approach that is not restricted to any gharana or to any particular form of music. These seven coordinates are:

- Voice training and voice culture: How a student should develop his or her voice as a voice that is his or her signature.

- Understanding frequencies and notes: A thorough awareness of both and their relationship with each other.

- Movement and connectivity of notes: The science of connecting one note to another, envisioning the route of the notes and the application of this knowledge to various kinds of music.

- The relationship between lyrics, literature and music: Understanding the content and value of lyrics, the relationship between the mind and the *swara* and the aesthetics of melody, word and intonation.

- *Tala* and *laya*: The art of taking time out of the space available and using it creatively while performing on stage and in life in general.

- Raga: Knowledge and understanding of the uniqueness of ragas and the raga system.

- Self-belief and humanism: Understanding the spirituality of music, the larger purpose of practising music and the values embedded in the ancient Sanskrit scriptures, especially the *Vedas* and the *Upanishads*.

An artiste needs at least 15 to 20 years of hard work and grooming. You have to start very young if you want to go far. The standards of excellence that I expect a performer to reach cannot be reached if proper music education is not given from an early age. My belief in bringing the whole world into an open-ended classroom for a student, instead of closing the room and shutting the student inside, has paid rich dividends in the form of some very creative, very brilliant students.

We talk of training the mind to bring it under control. We talk of training the body to make it respond better to a variety of situations. We talk of training our hands so that they can do what we want them to do, drawing or sculpting, for example. But we rarely talk about training the voice. We only talk of

'learning to sing'. Shrutinandan believes that people are missing a step here. Most music classes in homes, schools and more formal or more advanced vocal music training institutions only focus on tuning the voice and the best possible replication of a phrase or a set of phrases that we call a composition or a song. Vocal music training in the Shrutinandan way, involves crafting the voice in such a manner that it responds to the commands of the singer and moves in the way that he or she wants it to. This practice is incomplete without knowing the final destination, the right resting places on the way and the power that needs to be put into the journey at every step, that is, how to intonate and project each note, when journeying within a musical phrase.

Instead of just repeating what I sing, I ask students to complement the phrase that I have sung. This encourages the students to think. I did the same with Kaushiki when she was a child. In Shrutinandan we do the same thing with everyone. This enables a child to create his or her own musical persona. It creates disciples who have not only learnt deeply from their gurus, but have also found their originality. This creates self-respecting musicians and humble human beings.

Shrutinandan's 10th year celebration at Netaji Indoor Stadium, Kolkata

ga

Music is not property that one inherits from earlier generations. Excellence in music cannot be guaranteed by any claims to heredity. Being god-gifted is not enough, though it helps. It also helps if one belongs to a family with a good musical ambience, because a child feels motivated to learn. None of this, however, guarantees results. None of this can substitute the hard work and dedication that is needed to shape a musical ability into achievement. Reaching success is easy but staying there is difficult. Living up to expectations is the real challenge. For this, one not only needs mastery over technique but also integrity of character and a sense of aesthetics. There are no shortcuts in creating anything of enduring value.

> I see a lot of gifted aspiring singers on the scene now but they can't survive without hard work. I started learning music like any other student, but gradually I realised that I didn't want to just learn it … I wanted to live it. Music is the oxygen that I need to survive.

While it is true that every gharana has a dominant *bhava* (a word that can be translated to mean emotion, disposition or feel) it is equally true that even within a gharana, the dominant *bhava* can differ from practitioner to practitioner. For instance, the dominance of *veera bhava* (emotion of valour) in Ustad Ashiq Ali Khan of Patiala gharana's *gayaki* is replaced by the dominance of *shringara bhava* (emotion of love) in the *gayaki* of Ustad Bade Ghulam Ali Khan Saheb. The dominant *bhava* of a singer or for that matter any artiste in any field of art is like the main port of anchorage from where the artiste sets out on many a journey marked by many a *bhava*. Pandit Ajoy Chakrabarty's *gayaki* has a dominant *bhava* too—*ananta bhava* or the emotion of infinity.

It was this infinity that Rabindranath Tagore thirsted for, when he wrote the poem 'Aami chanchal he, aami sudurer piyasi' (I am ever on the move, I thirst for infinity). To revel in this *bhava* of infinity is every child's birthright. Pandit Ajoy Chakrabarty believed that decadent systems had snatched this birthright from a student of music.

FACING PAGE
(above): Pandit Ajoy Chakrabarty conducting classes at Shrutinandan
(below): Pandit Ajoy Chakrabarty with Amal Chatterjee (left) and Indranil Bhaduri (right)

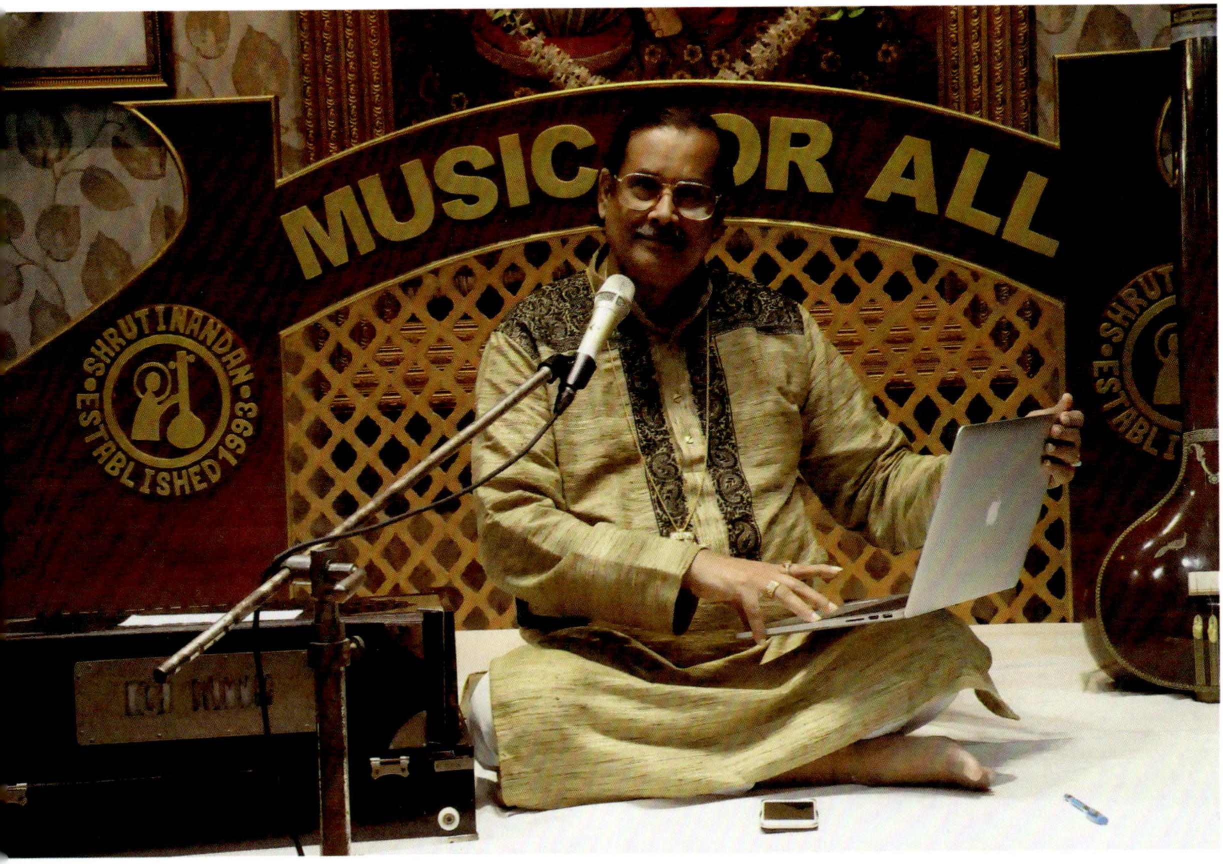
MUSIC FOR ALL
SHRUTINANDAN
ESTABLISHED 1993

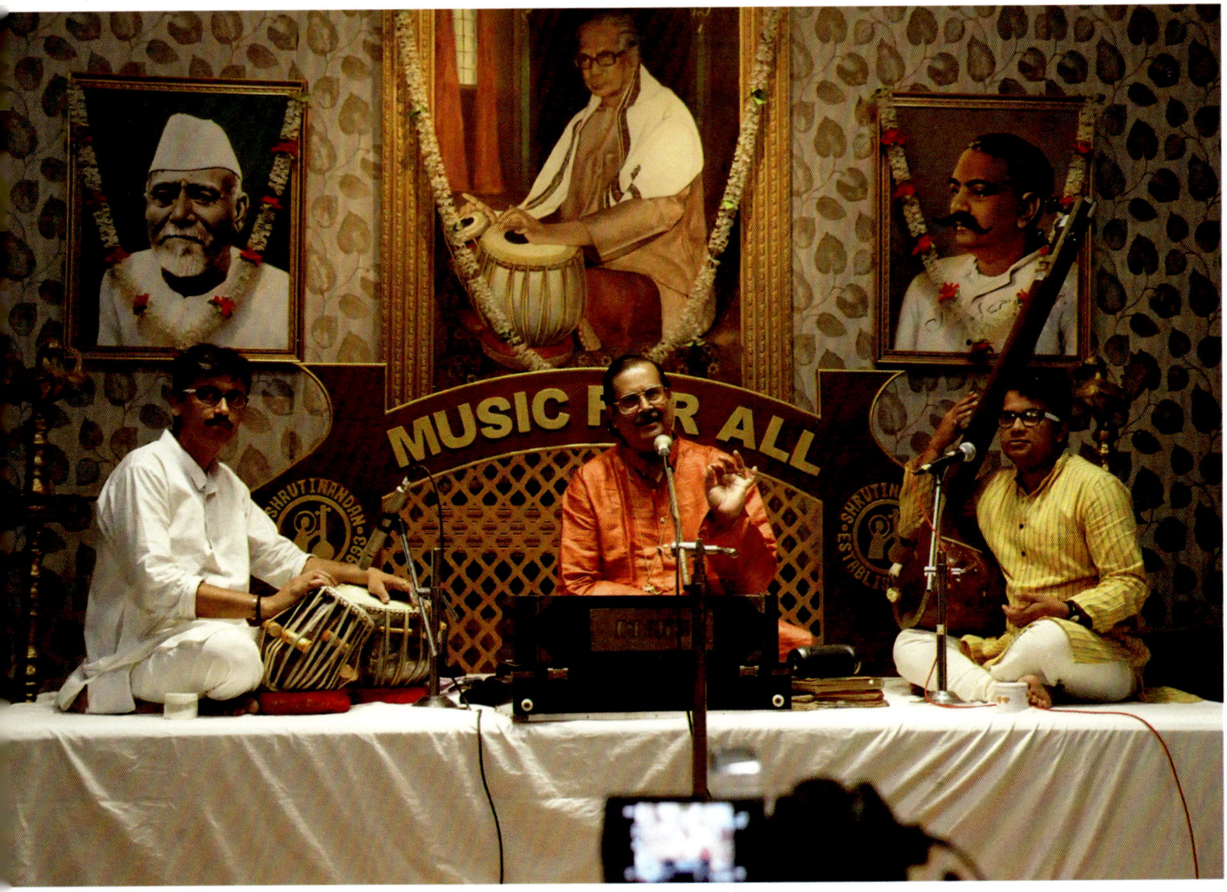
MUSIC FOR ALL

Clockwise from above:
Pandit Ajoy Chakrabarty with Shankar Mahadevan
and young students; Shrutinandan honours Guru
Jnan Prakash Ghosh; performing at his 60th anniversary
concert; performing with Chandana Chakrabarty;
Saraswati Puja at Shrutinandan; conducting a class
at Shrutinandan; conducting an online music class;
Guru Jnan Prakash Ghosh Sanctum at Shrutinandan

Chandana and Ajoy Chakrabarty with students

Tagore has also written, 'the greatest of educations for which we came prepared is neglected, and we are made to lose our world to find a bagful of information instead.' Pandit Ajoy Chakrabarty felt that this was also happening in the field of music. He had taken his call. He would not exchange his love for music for any tradition that throttled freedom of musical expression. Nor would he let anyone stop him from teaching children to revel in the *ananta bhava* of musical infinity.

A creative person can see the different components of the whole and take them apart to put together a different whole. At the same time, he or she can see the oneness that can be created from that which is lying around in bits and pieces. Most importantly, a creative person can see that which others cannot. Those who cannot see what he or she

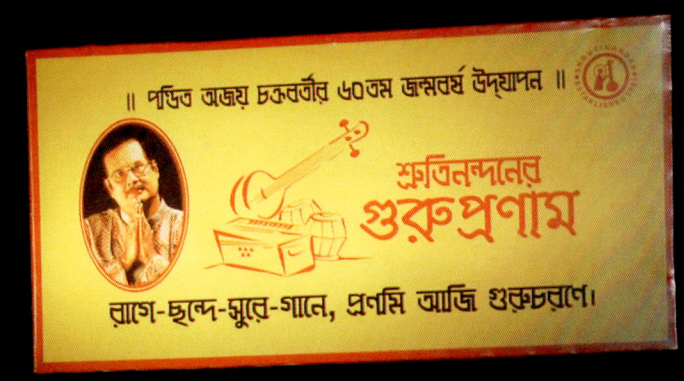

Commemorative concert by students
of Shrutinandan on
Pandit Ajoy Chakrabarty's
60th birthday

CD covers of 'Hey Ram'
and 'Gadar'

sees are at a loss to understand what is being done and why. The creation of Shrutinandan was one such thing. Pandit Ajoy Chakrabarty left most people who did not understand him, to live with their thoughts and confusions, and moved on. For a musician, there is only one way to move—indulging in more music. In Pandit Ajoy Chakrabarty's case this meant music of many more kinds for more and more people.

In 1999, maestro-composer Ilayaraja created a roller-coaster classical track based on Raga *Hamsanadam* for a song titled 'Isaiyil Thodanguthamma' for Indian superstar Kamal Hasan's film *Hey Ram*. It needed a classical singer with a tiger-like grip on *laya* to do justice to it. Ilayaraja asked Pandit Ajoy Chakrabarty to render the iconic song in Tamil and Hindi (for the Tamil and Hindi versions of the film). The song remains etched in the memories of music lovers. *Hey Ram* was released at the turn of the millennium, in February 2000.

The same year saw the Government of India conferring the apex cultural recognition, the Sangeet Natak Akademi Award on Pandit Ajoy Chakrabarty for excellence in Hindustani classical music.

Meanwhile, to add colour to the melodious mix of forms that Pandit Ajoy Chakrabarty represented, the song *'Aan milo sajna'* rendered with Begum Parveen Sultana for Bollywood's box-office record-breaking film *Ghadar* had become very popular in 2001. It was the same year in which Pandit Ajoy Chakrabarty held the audience spellbound on India Gate lawns, late on a winter night in New Delhi with his magical unfoldment of raga *Maru Behag*. The lucky ones who heard his *'Ratiyan hamaar bairan'* at Music Today's Swar Utsav 2001 relived the delight of its classicism in the album that was released the following year. The night also resounded with a mesmeric rendition of Ustad Bade Ghulam Ali Khan's iconic *dadra 'Yaad piya ki aaye'* and the *thumri 'Kaa karun sajani aaye na baalam'*. The music label aptly named the album *Ajoy Chakrabarty: Scaling Classical Heights*.

Scaling new heights, changing mindsets, riding many boats …. what to others looked like a hundred journeys was just

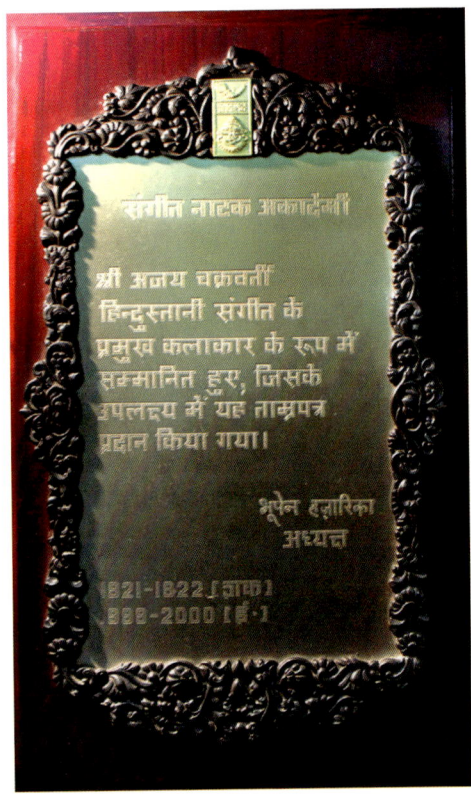

Sangeet Natak Akademi Award bestowed on Pandit Ajoy Chakrabarty

one yatra for Pandit Ajoy Chakrabarty. One music, one pilgrimage, one journey within. In 2002 he echoed these thoughts in a unique rendition of Tagore's *'Aami chanchal he, aami sudurer piyasi'* in the album *Ajana Khanir Notun Moni* (A new gem from an unknown mine), almost a century after Tagore wrote the song. Purists of Rabindra Sangeet had much to say but Pandit Ajoy Chakrabarty had heard it all before, like Tagore had heard criticism of so many of his works in his lifetime. The album has grown into a milestone since then.

ma

Love for music has many colours, vocal music is just one of them. Instrumental music, music direction, music recording, music production, music education, music marketing, music sales, music-related technologies ... the palette is huge. To each his own colour! To each his own music!

Pandit Ajoy Chakrabarty's son Ananjan also grew up in the same milieu as his elder sister Kaushiki. About 10 years younger than his sister, Ananjan was the first student at Shrutinandan. The greatest fan of his sister's singing, Ananjan has also imbibed the family's fascination for music. But no two people are identical. Few people know this better than Pandit Ajoy Chakrabarty. His entire system of music education pivots around harnessing a child's uniqueness.

Ananjan Chakrabarty with his father

Ananjan was six years old when Shrutinandan was inaugurated and he joined as its first full-fee paying student. In fact, as his father, I sometimes also paid a late fee for missing the deadline. Ananjan had a very playful mind, full of many interests. Kaushiki on the other hand was very focused and single-minded in her pursuit of music. At first,

I thought it was a weakness but with time I realised that it was another kind of strength. Ananjan learnt music at Shrutinandan for 10 years.

Every parent wants to see more than a little bit of himself or herself in his or her child. It was instinctive for Pandit Ajoy Chakrabarty to do so too. But in dealing with so many children he had come to respect that a parent or

Ananjan with Ustad Zakir Hussain

Ananjan practising music

a teacher enables a child to develop much better, if he or she encourages the child to explore within.

Chandana and I had been brought up in another world. On our part, we needed to learn to accept that. It was not easy.

It is a common parental weakness to see the fulfilment of their dreams in their children. My father had done that. It had worked to my advantage because my dream was not different from his dream. What if my dream had been different? What if I did not have the attributes that my father believed that I did? What would I have gone through then? These are important questions. I advise parents who bring their children to Shrutinandan with the same honesty with which I tried to understand what Ananjan had in him, where Ananjan wanted to go and what would give Ananjan lasting happiness.

In many cases *parivar parampara* or family traditions have disintegrated, because it was assumed that a great ustad's child would or must also grow up to become a great ustad, singing the same compositions or playing the same instrument with the same flourish. Success is achieved if the light of inherent potential is lit with the flame of love. To do this it is important to identify the work that can give the doer enjoyment for all times. Sometimes an inheritance needs to be put aside or remixed to create a vibrant new colour on the palette.

With Pandit Ajoy Chakrabarty and Kaushiki Chakrabarty singing hour after hour to perfect their vocal skills, and his mother teaching so many students every day, young Ananjan had a front row seat in the amphitheatre of musical experiences. He grew up listening to not just his celebrity father and sister, but many other stalwarts and legends with whom he came in contact by virtue of his being positioned where he was in life. The ear, unlike the lips, is not selective. What goes in, goes in and stays somewhere. An ocean of music must have gone into little Ananjan's head and heart. However, unlike his father and sister, Ananjan had no intention of echoing it back in the way they enjoyed doing it.

Instead of becoming a bird flying far and high in the sky of music, Ananjan wanted to swim in the ocean of music like a fish—studying the ocean, mapping its waters, diving and exploring the depths and shallows of its sights and sounds and creating new views and melodies. This was a very different perspective. Pandit Ajoy Chakrabarty realised that for Ananjan music was a larger, more fluid and a more experimental experience. Ananjan enjoyed being the experiencer and the deliverer of the experience rather than being one of the sources of the experience. Ananjan enjoyed interpreting the experience. This was the most expressive colour of Ananjan's love for music.

Understanding this was very important for us, because understanding Ananjan was going to have a bearing on our understanding the future of some other children, who could be in a similar situation.

Having learnt tabla for some time from Mallar Ghosh, Guru Jnan Prakash Ghosh's son, Ananjan had a very good sense of rhythm. He also had a flair for music composition. Even as a teenager he asked me questions that were more about the construction and texture of music rather than its performance. He was sure that he would not take up a career in singing, but he wanted to be in the world of music and also excel in it.

One thing was clear in our minds. If Ananjan desired to have a life in music, then it had to be his call and not ours. But he was young and he needed advice. We would be failing in our duty if we did not advise him honestly and objectively. I had to forget for a while that I was Ananjan's father or how much I loved him and wanted him to be near me. He needed to forget for some time that he was classical vocalist Ajoy Chakrabarty's son. I explained this to him. I explained this to Chandana too.

It was easier said than done. We had a heart-to-heart talk over more than one session. Finally, Ananjan decided to shift base to Mumbai and learn Sound Engineering from Shri Daman Sood, India's famous sound engineer at Digital Academy.

Recording is an early 20th-century phenomenon but no other aspect of the music industry has grown to impact music as much as the art and science of sound recording and sound design. Pandit Ajoy Chakrabarty's generation was actually the first generation that had the advantage of measuring the quality of their own renditions by comparing

Ananjan in his recording studio

them with the renditions of stalwarts by listening to their audio recordings. Before his generation, artistes did not have to give much thought to the creative demands or the technical challenges that one has to face in a recording studio.

The environment in an audio studio is so different from the environment of a concert. It takes time to get used to it. I know many successful concert artistes who even to this day feel out of sync in a recording studio. Many artistes, especially classical and folk artistes are uncomfortable when they have to sing or play to the accompaniment of a prepared music track. At the same time, there are classical artistes who have mastered the art of recording too, but they are in a minority.

I remember the day I stepped into a recording studio for the first time. Guru Jnan Prakash Ghosh was a master of recording aesthetics and sound engineering. I had heard so much about different aspects of audio recording from him and I had been singing for years but even then, I suddenly found myself in a world that was alien to me.

Is it not strange that we give years and years to learning music but forget to make friends with the one instrument that finally presents our voice to the world? I am talking of the microphone.

A microphone lays bare many of the weaknesses in a voice. An audio recording exposes these even more. What would otherwise pass over with a minimal reaction from a connoisseur in a live concert never gets passed off in a recording. An audio recording challenges a singer's accuracy in projecting notes and handling breath, intonation and throw of voice.

Talking of microphones and sound systems, I remember a very special concert organised by Uttar Pradesh Tourism with the permission of the Archaeological Survey of India in the courtyard of Fatehpur Sikri, the beautiful 16th century ghost city, which was once the capital of the great Mughal Emperor Akbar. Here, in the middle of a small reservoir called Anup Talao, Akbar's legendary court singer Tansen sat and sang for the emperor. The stage was set at the same place where Tansen is believed to have performed. Only Pandit Bhimsen Joshi had sung there before. There was a huge audience, numbering a few thousand at least. I started singing...

It was a full moon night. It was the brightest moon of the year, Sharad Poornima—the auspicious day on which Bengalis worship Lakshmi, the goddess of prosperity. It is said that Sharad Poornima is the best night to see the

Ananjan with his father in his recording studio

Taj Mahal, because the moon that night reaches its zenith in the sky and so, for some time, the Taj Mahal does not have a shadow. That night, a few miles from the Taj Mahal, as the full moon rose in the sky, Ajoy Chakrabarty requested the organisers to switch off the lights and the sound system. In one stroke of the switch, the night got time-warped in the ambience in which Emperor Akbar must have enjoyed Tansen's performances. The *Darbari Kanada* that Pandit Ajoy Chakrabarty sang thereafter was the last concert held at Anup Talao in Fatehpur Sikri!

The acoustics of Anup Talao surprised me. Every note reached every part of the courtyard. It was an unearthly feeling. I think a few ghosts of Akbar's ghost city must have joined the audience. Maybe the soul of *Sangeet Samrat* Tansen made the magic happen.

The chances of another concert at Anup Talao are rare but the existence of so many such acoustically perfect, ancient and medieval structures in India points to the high sense of acoustic engineering that has existed in India since ancient times. Sound has always

Ananjan mixing music in his recording studio

been treated as a form of Divine Truth in this land: *Naada. Naada Brahman.*

In the modern world of music, every vocalist or instrumentalist needs to have at least a basic understanding of microphone usage and music recording techniques. Knowing that it was not possible for everyone to have access to a recording studio, I had planned to have an audio studio in Shrutinandan to give the students an opportunity to experience and understand the dynamics of song recording.

With Ananjan's decision to become a sound engineer and sound designer, I put my plan in motion. I requested Shri Daman Sood to design a state-of-the-art audio studio in Shrutinandan. He agreed and I am extremely grateful to him, because he helped us to create one of the finest audio studios in the eastern region without any financial interest whatsoever.

pa

Shrutinandan's recording studio was blessed by the presence of Ustad Zakir Hussain

When the studio was about to go to the design table, the unexpected happened. The pace that Pandit Ajoy Chakrabarty had set for himself, the packed concert schedule that he had been following to raise funds for Shrutinandan, combined with the general rigours of a busy artiste's life took a toll on his health. In March 2009 Pandit Ajoy Chakrabarty suffered a cerebral stroke.

I was scheduled to perform at the Jai Bharati-IV festival at Chinmaya Mission in New Delhi but could not make it for the show. I was in the ICU lying on the edge of the mountain called life. When I regained consciousness and later recovered enough to receive news from outside, I was told that in my absence Swami Tejomayananda, the worldwide head of Chinmaya Mission had presented a devotional music evening himself. Like most of life, every concert is pre-ordained and has the artiste's name written against it.

With the prayers and good wishes of thousands of people I started on my road to recovery. As usual, I was in no mood to waste time. But I also knew that things happen when they are destined to. It took some time. Such a close encounter with death was to leave its mark for ever on my philosophy of life and music—a mark of positivity.

Shrutinandan's studio was finally inaugurated in November 2011 by Pandit Shiv Kumar Sharma and blessed by the presence of Ustad Zakir Hussain.

I couldn't have asked for more. The two have been like elder brothers to me. They had seen me grow from my early days. I will never forget the memories of our road journeys with other artistes to so many remote destinations in India to spread the joy of classical music amongst the masses in line with the mission of ITC-SRA.

Between them, these two classical music giants of the world had left no form of music untouched by their excellence. Classical, light classical, jazz, fusion, film … they had hallmarked every form of music with their fantastic body of recorded work. Most importantly, both Ustad Zakir Hussain and Pandit Shiv Kumar Sharma are people who have inspired me by personal example to stand steadfast in my belief in a non-compartmentalised approach to music education.

I find great joy in learning about the latest technologies and trends in music recording, production and marketing from my son Ananjan today. It is a wonderful feeling. Learning from youngsters is so energising.

The openness to learn from everyone all the time has been a continuous theme in Pandit Ajoy Chakrabarty's evolution as a complete musician. He has always made a conscious effort to prevent his mind from getting stuck in the rusted spokes of the 'I know it' wheel.

Many years ago, I heard Zainul Abedin, who was then a young ITC Sangeet Research Academy scholar and a disciple of Ustad Latafat Hussain Khan singing a *bandish.* It was beautiful.

Left to right: Pandit Ajoy Chakrabarty receiving the Padma Shri award from then President Pratibha Patil (2011), receiving the Best Male Playback Singer award from then President R. Venkataraman (1990), at the Kumar Gandharva Samman presentation (1993), being honoured with an Honorary Doctorate at the University of Kalyani, receiving the Tansen Award and receiving the Gold Disc Award from Lata Mangeshkar

I asked Zainul to teach me the *bandish*. Zainul was taken aback and said, 'What are you saying? Who am I to teach you? Please do not say teach.' I remember telling him that whatever word one may use for it—teach or take—in the end it is learning. Whatever is good and touches the mind and the heart should be learnt with humility, regardless of from whom or where it emerges. Learning, like music, cannot be compartmentalised.

In 2011, the Government of India awarded Pandit Ajoy Chakrabarty the Padma Shri, one of the highest national honours in the country for his contribution to Indian classical music.

When I went to receive the award from the President of India, at Rashtrapati Bhawan in New Delhi, my memories went back full circle to a busy platform of the railway station in Delhi in 1972, when I visited the city for the first time to appear for my National Scholarship Examination. I did not know anyone in the city, not a soul. Clutching a tin suitcase, I positioned myself at the door of the bogie, as the train entered the platform, to try to identify a man called Subhrata Sen, whose reference I had got from a neighbour in Shyamnagar. I saw a man who was a few years older and many inches shorter than me, waving at me. I don't know how 'Nau Da' (as I later got to

Left to right: Some of the many awards of Pandit Ajoy Chakrabarty

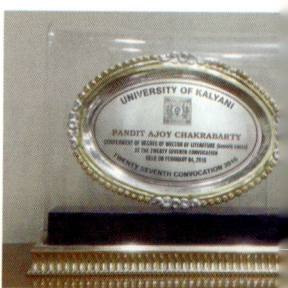

call him) recognised me. He took me to his modest home in the government quarters in Moti Bagh and hosted me like he would host a music superstar. I was overwhelmed. On that trip, I made some friends for life—Siddhartha Dasgupta, Niloy Sen and Dilip Sen. I can neither forget nor repay the selfless love that I received from Nau Da over the years on successive trips to Delhi. The Padma Shri took many years. Nau Da had passed away by then.

When I went to receive the award, I invited Siddhartha to join me and Chandana for the award ceremony in Rashtrapati Bhawan. His presence was symbolic of the presence of all the people whom I wanted to thank, in reaching wherever I have been able to reach in life.

Singing the glory of Indian classical music in some of the most prestigious venues of the world, including Carnegie Hall, the Kennedy Centre, New Orleans Jazz Preservation Hall in the USA (where he was honoured with the award of the Golden Key to the city of New Orleans), Royal Albert Hall and Queen Elizabeth Hall in UK and Theatre de la Ville in France, Pandit Ajoy Chakrabarty has travelled a long way to rendezvous with the *swara*. This journey has been marked by many milestones in the receiving of immense love and admiration across the world and many awards too.

Pandit Ajoy Chakrabarty was honoured with the Government of Madhya Pradesh's Tansen Award in 2015. He also received the Guru Jnan Prakash

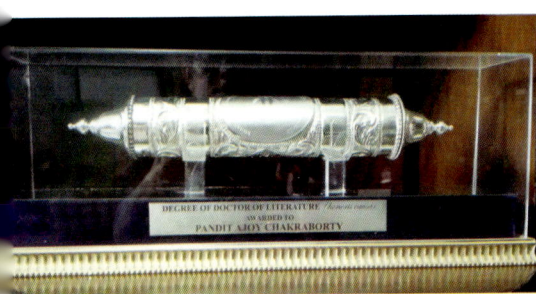

Pandit Ajoy Chakrabarty receives the 'Bishesh Sangeet Samman' on behalf of Pandit Jnan Prakash Ghosh

Ghosh Lifetime Achievement Award in the same year.

In 2016, Shrimati Mamta Banerjee, the Chief Minister of West Bengal honoured him with the Banga Bibhushan Award and the Maha Sangeet Samman, the highest awards in the state.

Pandit Ajoy Chakrabarty has also been honoured with honorary doctorates (DLitt) by the Indian Institute of Engineering Science and Technology (IIEST) Shibpur and Kalyani University in West Bengal.

Pandit Ajoy Chakrabarty being honoured by IIEST Shibpur

dha

Drawing lines that divide is mankind's oldest pastime. Music has been classified into innumerable categories too. We have even categorised our perceptions about learning and practising music. Music has even been classified on a scale of difficulty and ease of rendering. Music's compartmentalisation into stereotyped genres has destroyed its core. Classical musicians in general do not associate with popular music and those who are into popular music, like pop, rock, folk and playback singing, do not generally relate to classical music.

I fell in love with music long before I had heard the name of any classical artiste. I can say that my love for music was not ignited by any classical vocalist. It was the call of the divine—the kirtans and bhajans that my parents sang when I was a child. It was the call of the earth—the folk songs that I heard when I travelled by train or boat. It was the call of life—the songs of Tagore, Nazrul, contemporary poets and composers and also Bangla and Hindi film hits. I was very lucky to have had good guides. They did not ask me to shut my ears to any kind of music. They explained to me that there was one

Lata Mangeshkar receives a lifetime achievement award from Pandit Ajoy Chakrabarty

great mountain from where all these calls echoed—the wondrous mountain of *raga sangeet*—and that without making an effort to climb this mountain it was impossible to appreciate or render the many smaller echoes of the larger sound called raga.

The magical mountain of the raga is a kingdom in itself where every subject is equal. Everyone is a king. Everyone is happy. Everyone sings. The only law in this kingdom is 'Love for Music'. That is the reason why, when Pandit Ajoy Chakrabarty was looking for a tagline for Shrutinandan, he chose the phrase 'A Musical Kingdom'.

It is said that when Sri Krishna decided to give up his earthly incarnation and to return to his cosmic abode, Uddhava, his childhood friend, asked him who would now show the way after Krishna's departure. In answer, Sri Krishna is said to have narrated an incident from one of his past lives, in which he had as many as 24 gurus, including some objects, animals and birds too.

Pandit Ajoy Chakrabarty can count more than 24. He has a put up a beautiful poster in Shrutinanadan that displays the portraits of artistes from different genres from whom, and from whose music, he had the opportunity to learn something. The list starts with a portrait of Guru Jnan Prakash Ghosh and ends with a portrait of Bollywood legend Asha Bhonsle. Some names and faces have to be added to it…

> Just like there are geniuses and stalwarts amongst performers of *raga sangeet* there are geniuses and stalwarts in other forms so music too. I have learnt so much from them. I can count more than 24 gurus.

> Who in the world of *raga sangeet* could have taught me what I learnt

while singing for Ilayarajaji? There is so much to learn when you experience someone like Uttam Singhji arranging a composition like '*Aan milo sajna*', which he asked me to sing for the film *Ghadar*. When I was singing it, I knew and respected the fact that he was also the composer of the super-hit music of the Shahrukh Khan film *Dil To Pagal Hai*.

Can we talk of *Dil To Pagal Hai* without bowing our head to the great Lata Mangeshkarji, who provided the playback for its college-going heroine at the age of 68? How many artistes in the world can do that so convincingly? I have enjoyed the bounty of interacting with her. I would not hesitate to say that I consider her as one of my gurus. I have followed her music, and that of her sister, respected Asha Bhonsleji, since childhood. It was an honour to receive the Master Deenanath Mangeshkar Paritoshik Award for 2016 from Lataji and Ashaji.

While it is true that audio recording poses singing challenges, modern technology can clean your voice, make pitch corrections and do so many other things. Lataji and Ashaji did not have recourse to all this. They did not need to as their pitching was so brilliant. I once asked Lata Didi, 'When you move into the line of a song and move out of it there is a beautiful fade in and

Pandit Ajoy Chakrabarty and family members with Lata Mangeshkar

Top: *Pandit Ajoy Chakrabarty with Asha Bhosle and Kumar Bose (second from right)*
Above: *Pandit Ajoy Chakrabarty and Kaushiki with Ashaji*

fade out effect in your singing in many songs. How do you do it?' She was amused and showed me how she did it, not just in recordings but also in live concerts. I later tried the technique to good effect in some of my concerts.

How many singers with years of *raga sangeet* training can match Ashaji's perfection or Kishore Kumar's soulful magic and natural grasp of the *swaras*? Not only that, there is so much *raga sangeet* actually embedded in some of their greatest songs. Where does one draw the dividing line?

I was a very serious student of *raga sangeet*, doing long hours of *riyaaz* under Guru Jnan Prakash Ghosh, when Kishore Kumar's songs in films like *Khamoshi, Safar* and *Amar Prem* drenched me with their brilliant rendition, their lyrics and compositions. I could never draw the line. Guruji also never wanted me to. In fact, he encouraged me to do just the opposite. I never got a chance to meet Shri Kishore Kumar. He was a great inspiration in my growing up years and remains so to this day.

'*Kuchh to log kahenge, logon ka kaam hai kehna*' (People will always have something to say; it is what people do). Pandit Ajoy Chakrabarty builds on this popular Kishore Kumar song from the film *Amar Prem* (composed

From the top: *Pandit Ajoy Chakrabarty with Satyajit Ray, Bijoya Ray and Rabi Ghosh; with his father and Manna Dey; with Rakhee Gulzar and his family; with Vyjayanthimala Bali*

Clockwise from top left:
Pandit Ajoy Chakrabarty with
Suchitra Mitra, Ghulam Ali,
Bhupen Hazarika, Ravindra Jain,
Hariharan, Daler Mehndi and
Dhirendra Chandra Mitra, his wife
and Pandit Manas Chakraborty

by Rahul Dev Burman) to demonstrate the melodic glory of Raga *Khammaj* in a unique concert that he does from time to time. Or for that matter, Bengal's iconic singer-composer Hemanta Kumar's composition '*Wo sham kucch ajeeb thi, ye sham bhi ajeeb hai*' (written by Gulzarji) that Pandit Ajoy Chakrabarty uses as a lyrical base to share the glory of Raga *Yaman*. When he was learning *Yaman* at the feet of Ustad Munawar Ali Khan in the early 1970s he had no idea that decades later he would be doing some very interesting concerts with Gulzarji himself.

Guru Jnan Prakash Ghosh always stressed on the importance of the clear projection of the lyrics of a composition. He drilled this sense of respect for lyrics in every disciple's mind. Guru Jnan Prakash Ghosh was an excellent lyricist himself. Bengal has been home to some great lyricists and poets. Outside Bengal the man who had always captured my imagination was Gulzar saheb.

My love for Rabindranath Tagore is also more than just a Bengali inheritance. I had even learnt some Rabindra Sangeet formally from famous Rabindra Sangeet artistes Shrimati Suchitra Mitra, Shri Subinoy Roy, Shrimati Sumitra Sen and Shrimati Maya Sen. I learnt Rabindra Sangeet from my wife Chandana too.

From the top: *Pandit Ajoy Chakrabarty with Shri Narendra Modi and Pandit Birju Maharaj; with Shri Jyoti Basu; with Shri Pranab Mukherjee; and with Shri Manmohan Singh*

Left: Ajoy and Chandana Chakrabarty with Shri Somnath Chatterjee and his wife, (middle) Ajoy Chakrabarty with percussion maestro Sivamani, and (right) with music director Uttam Singh

A man of many facets, Gulzar Saheb is also a great admirer of Gurudev Rabindranath Tagore's work and has done some very evocative transcreations of Tagore's poems in Urdu. So, I was absolutely thrilled when I was asked to share the stage with Gulzar Saheb in reciting and singing Rabindranath Tagore's poetry at the Bandish Festival hosted by the National Centre for Performing Arts, Mumbai in 2014. We explored the theme further in Abu Dhabi the next year. Every time I do a programme with Gulzarji, I am in awe of his fascinating command over his power of expression.

While on the subject of expression, let me add that lyrical expression is centric to the rendition of *thumri*. My guru, Pandit Jnan Prakash Ghosh was a master of this art. He taught me the finest nuances of *thumri*'s renditions. I later researched the subject thoroughly. But despite having researched the thumri so well, it was an eye-opener to perform in concerts with Pandit Birju Maharajji. *Thumri* is essentially a form of music that grew out of the world of classical dance, primarily kathak. So, when I experienced the great master evoking the *thumri*s with me on stage it was like he was taking me one step up into another world of expressive excellence. I have learnt so much from my interactions with Pandit Birju Maharajji.

The 13th century musician-poet Hazrat Amir Khusrau, who was a disciple of the great Sufi saint Hazrat Khwaja Nizamuddin Auliya, writes:

Left: *Pandit Ajoy Chakrabarty with Sandhya Mukherjee and Usha Uthup, (middle) with L. Subramaniam and his wife Kavita Krishnamurthy, and (right) with Ex Governor Shri Shyamal K. Sen*

'Oonchi dyodhi mere Khwaja ki mose chadho utaro na jaaye!

Keh do mere Khwaaja se mori baiyyaan pakad le jaaye!'

In essence, Hazrat Amir Khusrau is saying, 'My *khwaja* is at a higher level than I am and I find it difficult to climb the steps that lead to him. So please tell him to hold my hand and raise me up.'

Who will give this hand-holding to music audiences? A listener of Hindi film music can be deeply touched by Mohammad Rafi's *'Man tadpat hari darshan ko aaj'* or Kishore Kumar's *'Koi humdum na raha koi sahaara na raha'*, without knowing that the first song is based on Raga *Malkauns* and the second on Raga *Jhinjhoti*. But what if he is told about it? Will it not make a difference?

There are always two options in life. Sometimes you need both. One is to sit on the banks, cast a fishing line and wait for the fish to come to you and the other is to venture out to where the fish abound. There are sages who sit and meditate on life in a cave in the Himalayas believing that it is the call of the seeker of knowledge to come, or not come, to them. There are others who believe that it is their duty to pull every potential seeker up across the *'dyodhi'* or threshold by reaching out to them.

Pandit Ajoy Chakrabarty is a man on a mission, a mission to take the wondrous world of Indian classical music to more and more people in the country and on a mission to ignite the interests of younger generations in learning and

Left to right: *Shri Buddhadeb Bhattacharya, Mrinal Sen, Pandit Ajoy Chakrabarty, Ustad Amjad Ali Khan and Dr Taslima Nasreen*

appreciating Indian classical music in its various forms. He sees himself reaching out to them wherever they are. In achieving this, his biggest strength is his versatility, which enables him to relate the different forms of Indian music to their common fountainhead of the 12 notes. Few classical vocalists have ever had such a powerful grip on so many styles of Indian music, along with a deep understanding and powerful command over *raga sangeet*.

The problem is that there has been no nurturing of talent across genres. This has led to a situation where performers feel that they exist in mutually exclusive zones. There should be no dividing line. Whatever lines are there are like waves on the surface of the ocean. Underneath it is all one. One music. One world. One *sargam* with many different ragas.

We have built fences—fences of lack of mutual appreciation. Classical musicians are as responsible for making these fences as popular artistes. Classical artistes have to accept some of the blame for not having conveyed to the people in general how centric the raga system is to human living. If one human being looks upon the other as being inferior or uninteresting, then how can

***Clockwise from above:** Pandit Ajoy Chakrabarty and family with Mother Teresa; with Saurav Ganguly and his son; with Pankaj Udhas and Shirshendu Mukherjee; with mridangam maestro Karaikudi Mani*

there be a relationship of love and understanding between the two? This is true of music also.

Music is not an extra-curricular activity. Music is the mirror in which you can see your soul. No other education in the world can do that. Music should be as integral a part of everyone's life as the air they breathe. By mastering music, one can master oneself. In mastering your own self, you master all. I have seen and experienced this myself.

Music improves mental faculties and thinking abilities. When we practise music for three to four hours every day the mind is ready to take on the most challenging academic, professional and physical assignments too. Music

builds team spirit. One cannot perform well alone.

I am happy that most of my disciples have chosen to pursue music but it gives me even more happiness to know that their academic records are very good and that many of them are or have been on the top of their classes in colleges and universities.

Raga music needs to be taught to each and every child in school. Some may take it up more seriously than others but some kind of grounding in the basics of *raga sangeet* is very important to create new generations that may not practice it but can appreciate it.

Imagine an India steeped in *swara-consciousness* in which every child knows at least one raga!

A raga is like god. It is difficult to define, convenient to ritualise and impossible to cage. Like god, raga is an ideal that allows tremendous individualism of approach. Like god is the divine vehicle of man's faith, raga is the melodic vehicle of man's imagination. Like god it is also one with the five elements—earth, fire, air, water and space.

A raga blooms when the mind and speech are in perfect harmony. The Shadja or *Sa* (*Do*) is the earth or the sub-structure that holds a raga. Fired

by inspiration, the emotion of the raga is its cosmos. Its unending sky has a colour that is unique to it. In this huge expanse of space, an artiste plays with the raga. In doing so, he or she reaches out from his mind to the mind of the listener. This communication can be called successful only if the mood, the emotion and the colour of the raga is conveyed in all its purity and fullness. Like water, a raga can take many shapes and forms.

Raga is life. A raga cannot stay caged in a particular tradition or a particular time, though some hours, some seasons and some traditions do lend themselves better to the rendition of a raga than others.

A raga happens best when there is perfect communion between notes and thoughts ... between lyrics and melodic structure. I think we have neglected the lyrics part of raga *gayaki*. With a few exceptions, the focus of the great masters around whom gharanas were built, was on the rendition—the *gayaki*—and not on the compositions. There are very few compositions that bring out the character of a raga. It is a classical vocalist's duty to not just preserve old traditions but also nurture them by infusing newness that attracts and sustains interest in *raga sangeet* without compromising its classicism and content. Any kind of confinement

Clockwise from top left:
Pandit Ajoy Chakrabarty with Asha Parekh; with Chandana, Ananjan, Monami Ghosh, Bhaswar Chatterjee and his wife Nabamita Chatterjee; with Kamal Hassan, with Anup Jalota; with Kabir Suman; with Arijit; and with A.R. Rahman

Top row, from left: *Pandit Ajoy Chakrabarty with Jagjit Singh; with Asha Bhosle, Jitendra and Chandana; with shehnai maestro Ustad Ali Ahmed Hussain; with khanjeera maestro Bangalore N. Amrit, mridangam player Satish Kumar Patri, and a student Gurudutt A.K.*

Middle row, from left: *Pandit Ajoy Chakrabarty with Sonu Nigam; with Daman Sood and Ananjan; with Asit Desai and Smt. Hema Desai; with Pandit Arvind Parikh*

Bottom row, from left: *Pandit Ajoy Chakrabarty with Babul Supriyo and Chandana, with Pandit Ulhas Kashalkar and Smt Subhra Guha; with Shekhar Sen; and with Nachiketa*

is non-musical. The typical gharana system is confinement. Confinement of any kind cannot last long. Freedom is human beings' essential nature. More than love, more than respect, more than rewards, more than money everyone wants freedom. The highest form of freedom is freedom of expression. The highest form of freedom of expression is poetry and music.

In the final analysis what we call a gharana is a set of norms, traditions and expressions that have been shaped by and constantly added to by inspired individuals. When we think of this, we see that even gharanas emerged out of a desire for freedom—the desire of great artistes to perform their music and share it the way they wanted to.

It was in search of creative freedom that stalwarts moved from one place to another to find royal patronage in the princely states of India. Generations of possessive passing on of traditions turned gharanas into rigid fortresses that did not allow the freedom to venture far from their high walls.

The same desire for freedom of expression that saw the birth of gharanas is today seeing the lowering and disappearing of the walls that gharanas had built around them. Cause and effect are cyclic. From time to time this cycle of cause and effect also comes to its *nyasa swara*—the 'resting note' of a raga. The age of the gharanas was one such resting place for Indian classical music. Today, in the hands of inspired artistes and a new generation of excellent performers, Indian *raga sangeet* has moved out on an exploratory path yet again.

The creative movements that constitute *gayaki* or singing developed from the spontaneous movements that we see in nature. The swaying of a tree on a windy day, the flutter of leaves on branches, the flow of a mountain stream, the plunge of a waterfall, the rumble of clouds, the tweeting of birds, the deep stillness of a volcano, the ripple of waves. Every aspect of Indian *raga sangeet* has been cradled by nature—human and environmental; nature that is inside and outside man.

ni

Pandit Ajoy Chakrabarty presents former President APJ Abdul Kalam with a memento of Shrutinandan

Great masters have said that no artiste can sing a raga. All he or she can do is to surrender to a raga and then the raga will tell them what to do. This meditative surrender is a great expectation that a raga has from an artiste. It is this that makes Indian classical music divine.

Some people ask me, 'What is singing?' This is a very important question. We tend to dive straight into 'learning to sing' without trying to understand what singing is. Music has come to be perceived as one of the easiest careers to pursue. Nothing can be further from the truth.

Singing is a form of painting. It involves creating and seeing images. This painting is done on the canvas of the air around us. One can call it 'on-air painting'. A painter dips his brush in a patch of colour that he selects

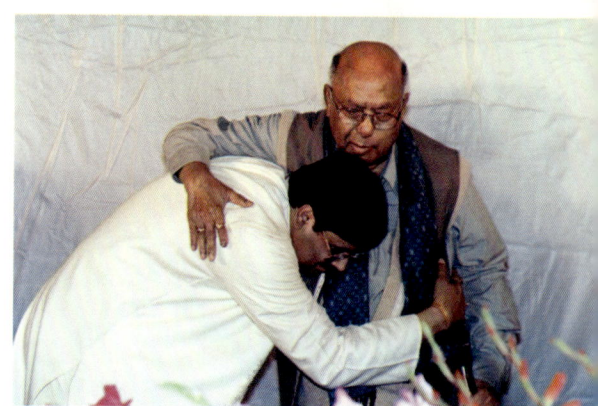

Clockwise from top left: Pandit Ajoy Chakrabarty with Pandit Ravi Shankar; with Ramkumar Chattapadhyay, Buddhadeb Bhattacharya, Ravi Shankar, Sukanya Shankar and Chandana; with Ali Akbar Khan; with Rajan and Sajan Misra; with Ustad Amjad Ali Khan; and with Girija Devi and Birju Maharaj

Top: *Pandit Ajoy Chakrabarty with Buddhadev Dasgupta and Anindo Chatterjee*
Middle: *with Sanjoy Mukherjee*
Above: *with Ustad Zakir Hussain and Kaushik Dutta*

from a palette of colours in his hand and applies it on the canvas in front of him. With each brush stroke the image takes shape. A classical singer dips the brush of his or her breath in the colours of the *swaras* or musical notes that are there on the palette of a raga to paint an image in the air. To do this on-air painting a singer uses a mix of different breath-strokes to create the desired image. This is true of all kinds of singing. In lighter forms of vocal music, we sometimes mix two or more sets of colours or ragas to create the desired image. Music is about seeing what one is singing. All music is 'singing', even when it is being played on an instrument. What we call *sur* or melody is therefore an audible image painted with a combination of notes or alphabets and note-combinations or words and phrases.

There is imagery in western classical music too—an imagery of the theme that the composer desires to convey. For example, Stravinsky's 'The Rites of Spring', Beethoven's 'Eroica' or 'Pastoral' symphonies, Vivaldi's 'Four Seasons' or Tchaikovsky's 'Pathetique', which he himself is believed to have themed into four movements: life, love, disappointment and death.

Imagery is ingrained in poetry. Lyrics lend imagery to songs. Even melody is many a time ingrained in poetry. In

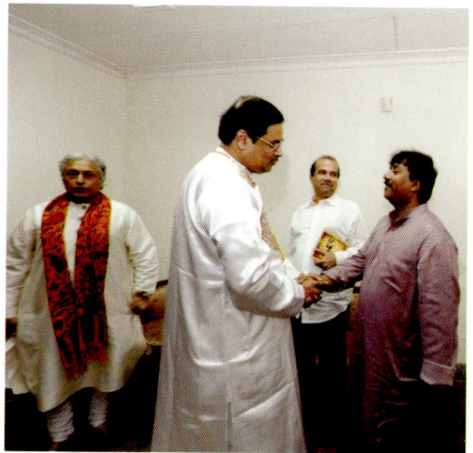

Left: *Pandit Ajoy Chakrabarty with Pandit Brij Bhushan Kabra, (right) with Ustad Amjad Ali Khan, Suresh Wadekar and Rashid Khan*

such cases additional melodisation can take a back seat because the words are melodic enough. The bottom line is that without imagery there can be no music. There are interesting differences though. For example, in a song the purpose of singing is to express the ethos of the lyrics, while in *raga sangeet* the purpose of singing a *bandish* (which is also a composition with words) is to express the ethos of the raga. Imagery is integral to both.

Seen as a whole, Indian music is a perfect combination of melody and harmonisation. A raga can be described as a disciplined way of expressing harmonies. It is this wholesomeness of music that Shrutinandan is focused on imparting. In an age where the average piece of music lasts four to five minutes, I look upon classical music like the great epics. It will endure forever, while waves of new music will come and go.

It is said that 'where science ends, philosophy begins'. If this is true then the philosophy of Indian classical music must be rooted in science. What is this science? Can it be researched? Can research be codified into a system that can be documented and applied at the individual level? Can this research be used to create scientific methods and tools for learning and appreciating *raga sangeet*? Pandit Ajoy Chakrabarty not only believes that this is possible but he has also taken a path-breaking step in making it happen—he has signed a landmark *sandhi* (a productive communion) with the Indian Institute of Technology, Kharagpur, as part of a larger national level initiative known as Operation SandHI (Science and

Pandit Ajoy Chakrabarty with his young students

Heritage Initiative) that grew out of the Government of India's acknowledgment of the urgent need to redefine and reconnect Indian knowledge sources and adopting an integrated knowledge systems approach, in which science and technology can become powerful agents for conserving India's cultural traditions. One of the most important focus areas of this project is Indian classical music. Research in this field is being helmed by Pandit Ajoy Chakrabarty.

I believe that we can bring about a renaissance in Indian classical music through a more objective and articulate understanding of the ragas. It is very unfortunate that there has been very little effort by maestros to articulate and archive the structure of ragas based on an intellectual understanding and scientific principles.

Every artiste has a unique style and this style is passed on to his or her students as best as the style can be verbally and aurally imparted and imbibed. In such a system, the *gayaki* remains confined to the guru and his or her disciples. It does not become a shared heritage that can be practised by others. In many cases, the *gayaki* itself died with the maestro. The same has happened with Indian classical instrumental music.

A 'charja' class by Panditji at Shrutinandan, which continued for 12 hours daily over three days. (Charja is an uninterrupted continuous association with the guru and extensive practice of music lessons during a period of three days to one week)

With IIT Kharagpur, Pandit Ajoy Chakrabarty will take a much needed relook at all aspects of Indian classical music following a truly holistic approach. The project will create a vast body of multimedia content and also study artificial intelligence techniques to evolve different ways of learning ragas. Exhaustive documentation of the pedagogy through recordings will help guide teachers and serious students. The evolution and development of *thumri gayaki* is also an important aspect of the project along with research on *omkar*-based music therapy. Shrutinandan's role is central to these activities.

I am already working on creating an archive of a 100 ragas. I am singing and recording them in groups, which will help create a much better and more holistic understanding of the ragas. The subtle nuances and the phraseology that differentiate similar *swara*-content ragas are being documented. Every detail will be given an easily referable documentation, so that they not only become India's intellectual property but they can also be conveniently accessed from knowledge domains generations later.

The present generation's classical maestros are the last living repository of the huge universe of knowledge and practices that we know as Indian classical music. I have committed myself to the cause. It is not just my objective, I see this cause as my life itself. I hope I can play my part in ensuring that the universe of Indian classical music's heritage does not disappear into a black hole with the

Ajoy Chakrabarty singing a song for the film Shakha Proshakha, *in the presence of the Oscar winning director Satyajit Ray and Smt. Bijoya Ray*

Ajoy Chakrabarty and Chandana Chakrabarty with Gulzar

passing away of the present generation of musicians. What I want to do will not be possible without the grace of God and my gurus.

I can't, I don't know, I have no experience. These are the three great obstructive thoughts on the path of success. Pandit Ajoy Chakrabarty has never allowed them to make their home in his mind.

The *swara* and being subservient to the *swara* is the highest truth. It is the supreme truth that has been orchestrating itself since the birth of the cosmos. It is a living, pulsating entity. It is the nucleus of all energy. Can you hear it singing? It is saying, 'I am swara.

I am God. I am the indivisible truth. I am *"akshara"*. I am forever. You cannot divide me. I have endless forms. I am in each of them'.

As the *Chandogya Upanishad* says:

Om! Poornamadah, Poornam Idam, Poornaat Poornam Udachyate
Poornasya, Poornam aadaaya, Poornam Eva Avashishyate
Om Shantih! Shantih! Shantih!

The infinite is on either side. From the infinite, the infinite is being born.

From the infinite if we take away the infinite, what remains is infinite.

Let there be Peace! Peace! Peace!

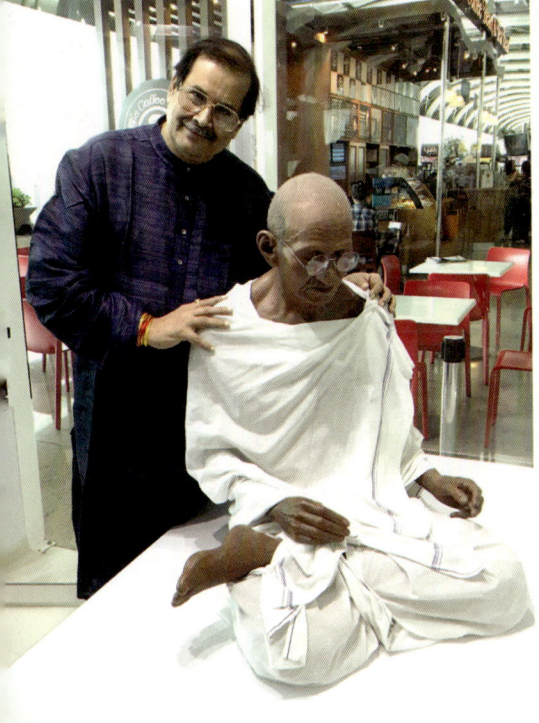

Top row, from left: Pandit Ajoy Chakrabarty with young Kaushiki; enjoying the company of birds at Avadhoota Datta Peetham, Mysore; on a foreign tour; in a concert at Gurupurnima

Bottom row, from left: Pandit Ajoy Chakrabarty with his wife Chandana Chakrabarty, partners in a musical journey; enjoying a game of billiards; playing carrom with friends; with a statue of Gandhiji, his inspiration; offering his tribute to Guru Jnan Prakash Ghosh

Sangeet Research Academy

Born in 1953 into a family deeply devoted to music, Ajoy Chakrabarty showed extraordinary promise in music since his childhood. He commenced his musical education under Shri Kanai Das Bairagi in 1960, continuing his general education concurrently. He won a record number of firsts in a number of music competitions, and later he joined the Rabindra Bharati University while taking training from Padma Bhushan Pandit Jnan Prakash Ghosh. Finally in 1971, Ajoy became a 'Ganda-bandh Shagrid' of Ustad Munawwar Ali Khan.

After a brilliant University record and award of the National Scholarship, Ajoy Chakrabarty was chosen by the Sangeet Research Academy in 1978 as a highly potent candidate for developing into a worthy performing artiste for the future of Hindustani vocal music.

Ajoy Chakrabarty has, in the last decade, been able to imbibe the rare values of Indian performance traditions. With the guidance of the experts and specialists at the Academy, he has conducted a serious personal enquiry into the finer aspects of the Patiala-Kasur gharana gayakee, immortalised by the late Ustad Bade Ghulam Ali Khan.

He has proved himself a worthy inheritor of the Patiala-Kasur tradition. He has established himself as a highly effective performer who gives due cognizance to the dual requirements of appeal and scholarship.

Ajoy has expanded his repertoire of compositions and ragas and has developed an ability and willingness to analyse, dissect and improve upon his own knowledge in keeping with the spirit of rationalisation nurtured and encouraged by the Sangeet Research Academy.

Ajoy Chakrabarty is awarded, today, the 23rd day of December 1988, the Fellowship of the Sangeet Research Academy. The Academy hereby formally grants him recognition as a successful Inheritor of Indian Classical Music traditions.

Ajit Haksar
Chairman

23rd December 1988
'Aldeen', Tollygunge, Calcutta

Vijay Kichlu
Executive Director

Fellowship of the ITC Sangeet Research Academy conferred upon Pandit Ajoy Chakrabarty in 1988

Padma Shri award conferred upon Pandit Ajoy Chakrabarty in 2011

Pandit Ajoy Chakrabarty seeks the blessings of Goddess Kali

Index

A

'Aan milo sajna' 183, 198
Abdul Kalam, APJ, *213*
Abedin, Zainul, 193
Abhogi, 138
Acharya, Srikanta, *135*
Adana, 128
Adda, 134
Aheer-Lalit, 128
Ajana Khanir Notun Moni, 183
Ajoy Chakrabarty: Live in Pakistan, 128
Akhtar, Begum, *86*, 125
album covers, *136-7*
Aldeen, 99, 106, 146, 151;
Ali Akbar Khan College of Music in San Rafael, 91
Ali, Ghulam, *202*
All India Radio, Kolkata, 45, 49
National Programme of Music in, 50
Amar Prem, 201
Amonkar, N. Vidushi Kishori, 124
Amrit, N. Bangalore, *210*
Andul Kali temple, 22
Arijit, *209*
audio recording, 188, 198
Auliya, Hazrat Khwaja Nizamuddin, 204
Aye na baalam, 129, 131

B

baanis 71, 108
Baby Jessica incident, 144
Badal-Benoy-Dinesh association, 16
Bado Ma, 18, 25, 31–2, 116
Bageshwari, 128–9
Bairagi, Kanaidas (Guru), 32, 35, *36*–8, 40–3, 48, 53, 56
Balamuralikrishna, M., *86*, *134*–5, *138*
Bali, Vyjayanthimala, *201*
Bandish Festival, 204
Bandishes, 24, 60, 70, 79, 108, 152, 162, 165, 172, 193–4, 216
Bandopadhyay, Ananda Gopal, *120*
Bandopadhyaya, Pulak, 125
Banerjee, Abhijeet, 50
Banerjee, Mamata, *127*, *196*
Banerjee, Prasun, 45, 50
Banga Bibhushan Award, *127*, 196

Bangla: compositions, 125; folk classics, 78; songs, 128, *see also* Tagore, Rabindranath songs
Barodekar, Vidushi Hirabai (Guru), *79*, 95, 110, *102*
Basu, Anil Krishna (father-in-law), *99*
Basu, Chandana. *See* Chakrabarty, Chandana Basu
Basu, Geeta (mother-in-law), *98*
Basu, Jyoti, *203*
Beethoven, 215
Best Male Playback Singer, 128, 142, 194
Bhaduri, Arun, 50, *108*, *120*, *147*
Bhaduri, Indranil, *176*
Bhaduri, Sishir, 30
Bhajans, 21, 28, 38, 40, 108, 133, 172, 197
Bhattacharya, Buddhadeb, *141*, 142, *206*, *214*
Bhattacharya, Uday as dhrupad Guru, 145
Bhava, 176, 180
Bhawan, Patha, 169
Bhorer shishir hoye, 125
Boral, Raichand, 116
Bose, Gobindo, 50
Bose, Kumar, *123*, *200*
Bose, Shyamal, 50, *148*
Bose, Sunil, 152
breath-strokes, 215
Burman, Rahul Dev, *86*, 203

C

Canada tours, 131
Carnatic music, 134–5
Carnegie Hall, New York, 135, 195
Chakrabarti, Arindam, 78, 145
Chakrabarty, Aghor, 61
Chakrabarty, Ajit, 15–19, 21–4, 26, 31, 51–2, 54, 56–8, 66, 81, 83, 91, 94, *102*–4, 113, 116; as first guru, 24; marriage with Jayanti Devi, 18; marriage with Mahamaya Devi, 17–18; settling in Shyamnagar, 19; as singer, 21; as teacher, 28; teaching music, *35*
Chakrabarty, Ajoy, *27*, *37*, *39-42*, 44, 53, 55, 62-3, *65*, *67-8*, *70*, 72, 75, 77, 79, 80-1, *89*, 95–6, *98*, *112*, 116–17, *120*–5, *130*, *132*–4, *138*, 140, 145, 148–50, 152, 163, 165, 178, 199–

207, 209–11, 213–16, 219, 223, 226; awards
of, 194; birth of, 18-20; with 'Bishesh Sangeet
Samman', 196; and Chandana Chakrabarty,
97, 100–1, 102, 105, 107–8, 110, 147, 157,
173; during concert, 168; with DLitt., 196;
with family members, 199, 207; father and
mothers, 20, (see also Bado Ma; Chhoto Ma);
with fish, 32; as Guru, 123, 154; with gurujis,
23; with IIEST Shibpur, 196; ITC Sangeet
Research Academy honours, 164; marrying
Chandana Basu, 97; music recordings by, 129;
with Padma Shri award, 194; as 'Pandit Ajoy
Chakrabarty', 132; practising with father, 26;
at Shrutinandan, 176

Chakrabarty, Ananjan, 156, 157, 158, 184,
186–7, 191, 209, 211; with father, 184, 189;
with Kaushiki, 159; as sound engineer and
designer, 191; with Zakir Hussain, 185

Chakrabarty, Chandana Basu, 78, 94, 97, 98–102,
107–8, 110, 144–7, 155, 157–8, 173, 178, 185,
187, 195, 209, 211, 214, 219, 223; and Ajoy
Chakrabarty, 180

Chakrabarty, Kaushiki, 79, 144–8, 151–5, 156-9,
169–70, 175, 184, 186, 200, 222; birth of, 146;
in concert, 168; with father as guru, 153–4;
ganda bandhan ceremony for, 151, 152;
marrying Desikan, 169; meaning Putul, (doll)
145; mother as guru of, 150; music education
of, 150–1; as scholar at ITC Sangeet Research
Academy, 153; touring USA, 152; university
education of, 169; young, 144, 146,
150, 168;

Chakrabarty, Sanjay, 124, 128

Chakraborty, Manas, 202

'charja' class, 218

Chattapadhyay, Ramkumar, 214

Chatterjee, Amal, 176

Chatterjee, Anindo, 40, 50, 140, 215

Chatterjee, Bhaswar, 209

Chatterjee, Nabamita, 209

Chatterjee, Somnath, and wife, 204

Chatterjee, Soumitra, 133

Chatterjee, Suniti Kumar, 49

Chhandaneer, 1989 128

Chhoto Ma, 18, 25, 31–2, 37, 116

Chitiriya Mata, 24

Choudhury, Ahindra, 28

Chowdhury, Amalendu Bikash Kar, 128

Chowdhury, Nirmalendu, 78

Chowdhury, Timir Roy, 124

classical: artistes, 188, 197, 206; maestros, 218

music, 54, 63, 66, 69, 73–4, 90, 94, 103,
123–4, 128, 193–5, 197, 205–6, 212, 216–18;
musicians, 78, 197, 206; vocalists, 49, 79, 121,
128, 197, 206

Commemorative concert by Shrutinandan, 181

Concerts, 51–4, 120–1, 125, 129, 131–2, 134–5,
138, 140, 148–9, 151–2, 157, 188–9, 193,
201, 203–4; in Delhi in 1982, 113, see also
international tours

creative movements, 212

curriculum, 28, 73

D

Da, Nau, 194–5

dadra, 57, 108, 128, 131, 172

Dagar Brothers, 88

Dagar, Fahimudddin (Guru), 109

Damini damke jiara mora larje, 131

Dasgupta, Buddhadev, 102, 215

Dasgupta, Siddhartha, 195

Deenanath Mangeshkar Paritoshik
Award, 198

Desai, Asit, 210

Desai, Hema, 210

Desikan, Parthasarathy, 158, 169

Devi, Girija, 102, 127, 214

Dey, Brojendra Kumar (Guru), 28

Dey, Krishna Chandra, 21

Dey, Manna, 86, 107, 125, 128, 201

Dikshitar, Muthuswami, 138

Dil To Pagal Hai, 198

Doorey aaro doore, 125

Dutta, Kanai, 50

Dutta, Kaushik, 215

Dutta, Sushim Mukul, 165

Dwarkin harmonium, 49

E

EMI Pakistan's landmark release, 128

Europe tour, 131, 149

F

Faiz, Faiz Ahmad, 122

Festival of India in US, 122, 135

Firoza, Begum, 127

first Guru, father as, 24–5, 150

first harmonium, 36

first home, 16

fish market, 31

folk songs, 197

G

Gadar, *182*
ganda bandhan, 69
Gandharva, Kumar, 124, 141
Ganguly, Hiru, *121*
Ganguly, Saurav, *207*
gayaki, 71, 77, 88, 93, 107–9, 113, 115, 122, 164,
    176, 208, 212, 217
gharana system, 70, 91, 93, 108–9, 171, 212
gharanas, 66, 69–71, 93, 108–9, 170–1, 173, 176,
    208, 212
Gharanedar taalim, 70
Ghatak, Ritwik, 87
Ghosh, Dwarakanath, 49
Ghosh, Gufam Premesh, *102*
Ghosh, Jnan Prakash (Guru), *23, 25, 32, 42–3, 48–*
    53, 55–8, 60–1, 66, *70, 73, 86,* 88, 91, 93–4,
    109–11, 113, *117,* 131, *140,* 151–3, 166, 196,
    203–4; and compositions, 49; as grandson of
    Dwarakanath Ghosh, 49; meeting, 48; with
    the Padma Bhushan, 50, 116; return of, 76;
    sculpture of, 50; shifting to Dixon Lane, 51;
    teaching in Pennsylvania University, 64; tribute
    to Guru, *223*
Ghosh, Jnan Prakash Ghosh Lifetime
    Achievement Award, 195–6
Ghosh, Lalita, 50, *108*
Ghosh, Mallar, 186
Ghosh, Monami, *209*
Ghosh, Mrinal Kanti, 21
Ghosh, Nikhil, 50
Ghosh, Rabi, *201*
Ghosh, Shankar, 50
Ghoshal, Anup, 128
Goa, 132
Goho, Jyoti, 87–9
great masters, 204, 208, 213
Guha, Subhra, *211*
Gulzar, 203–4
Gulzar, Rakhee, *201*
Gupta, Shyamal, 125
Guru Jnan Prakash Ghosh Puraskar, 50
guru(s), 32, 37–8, 63–5, 72, 74, 87–8, 90–1, 94–5,
    109, 111–13, 115–17, 153–5, 170, 198, (see
    also under separate entries); appointment as,
    116; fees 56, 76; nazrana or dakshina for, 69;
    and 'taxi-excuse', 56
guru-bhai, 32
Gurudutt A.K., *210*
gurukul, tradition, 93
guru-shishya relationship, 115

H

Hamir, 128, 164
Hamsadhwani, 138
hand-weaving loom, 23
Hari om tatsat, 129, 131, 138
Hariharan, *202*
harmonium, prohibition of, 50
Hassan, Kamal, *209*
Hazarika, Bhupen, *202*
Hey Ram, 182–3
HMV India, 128
Hussain, Ali Ahmed, *210*
Hussain, Zakir, *86,* 121, *130*–1, 154, 170, *185,*
    192–3, 215

I

Ichhapur, 80
Ichhapur Northland High School, 26, 28
Identity, 94, 104
IIT Kharagpur, 218
Ilayaraja, 182, 198
Imagery, 215–16
Indian music, 142, 206, 216
Individuality, 113, 115, 170
institution for children, 162, see also Shrutinandan
international tours, 120, see also Europe tour;
    Canada tour; Festival of India; USA tour
'Isaiyil Thodanguthamma', 182
ITC Company Limited's vision, 104
ITC Sangeet Research Academy (ITC-SRA), 44,
    90–1, 93–4, 96, 99, 103–4, 108–9, 113, 116,
    122–3, 139, 142, 145, 151–3, 163–4, 166, 193;
    Ajoy Chakrabarty as scholar of, 93, 103–4,
    109, 120, 123, 153; bond with, 70, 103–4,
    164; in Experts Committee 116; Fellowship
    of, *224;* as first scholar, 116; first scholar of,
    162; joined, 94, 103; in management of, 122;
    performing for, 120; stipend, 104
ITC Sangeet Sammelan, 94–5, *120, 122*–3

J

Jai Bharati-IV festival, 192
Jain, Ravindra, *202*
Jalota, Anup, *209*
Jasraj, Pandit, 124
Jitendra, *210*
Jog, V.G., 49, 116, *120*–1
Joshi, Bhimsen, *116,* 124, 188
Joshi, D.T., 116
jugalbandi, 24, 48, 50, 134–5; with Balamurali
    Krishna, 134

K

Kaare ba shonai, 125
Kabra, Brij Bhushan, *216*
kabuliwalah, 36–7
Kala Pahad, 28
Kali kirtans, 22, 40, 138
Kanaidas Bairagi (Master Moshai), 37–8, 41, 43,
    48–9, 51
Kanan, A.T. (Guru), 87–8, 95, *102*, 109, 116
Kanan, Vidushi Malavika (Guru), 109, 117
kantha-sujani weaving days, 24, 79
Karan, A., *102*
Karan-Arjun, 28
Kashalkar, Ulhas, *210*
Kasur-Patiala *gharana*, 43, 66, 113
Kasur-Patiala heritage, 91, 140
kathak, 204
Kaun jatan se preet nibhaaun, 131
Kedar, 128, 131
Khamoshi, 201
Khan, Abdul Karim, 61
Khan, Ali Akbar, *86*, *214*
Khan, Ali Baksh, 66
Khan, Alla Rakha, 154, 170
Khan, Ameer, *86*
Khan, Amir, 51
Khan, Amjad Ali, *206*, *214*, *216*
Khan, Ashiq Ali, 176
Khan, Baba Alauddin (Guru), 51, 63, *86*
Khan, Bade Ghulam Ali, *17*, *43–4*, 43–5, 61, 65–6,
    71, *75*, 77, *86*, 89, 93, *101*, 107–9, 113, 115,
    129, 131, *165*
Khan, Barkat Ali, 44, 66
Khan, Bundu, *86*
Khan, Dabir (Guru), 49
Khan, Faiyyaz, 93
Khan, Feroze (Punjab *gharana*) Guru, 50
Khan, Bismillah (Guru), *86*
Khan, Kale, 66
Khan, Khadim Hussain, *102*
Khan, Latafat Hussain (Agra *gharana*) Guru, *81*,
    88, 95, *102*, 110, 152, 193
Khan, Masit (Farukhabad *gharana*) Guru, 50
Khan, Munawar Ali, 45, 64–9, 71, 73, 76–7, 88,
    93–4, 109–11, *139–40*, 203
Khan, Nissar Husain (Guru), 95
Khan, Rashid, 96, *127*, *132*, *216*
Khan, Sagir (Guru), 49
Khan, Shahrukh, 198
Khan, Sultan, 129
Khan, Umar, 109

Khan, Vilayat, *86*
Khan, Vishar Hussain, *102*
Khan, Yunus (Guru), 95, 109, 117
khayal, 57, 103, 108, 133
khayal gayaki, 88
Khusrau, Hazrat Amir, 204, 205
kirtans, 21–3, 40, 197
Kolkata Music Circle, 87
Krishnamurthy, Kavita, *149*, *205*
Kumar Gandharva Samman, *141*, 141–2, 194
Kumar, Hemanta 128, 203
Kumar, Kishore 86, 201, 205

L

Lakshmi (cow), as fan, 30
Lakshmi Babu sweet shop, 41
Lalit, 128
'learning to sing', 175, 213
lyrics, 22, 24, 49, 58, 125, 172, 174, 201, 203, 208,
    215–16

M

Madhya Pradesh's Tansen Award, 195
Maha Sangeet Samman, 196
Mahadevan, Shankar, *178*
Mahamaya Devi, 17–18; elder mother, 18
Maharaj, Birju, *203*, 204, *214*
Maharashtra, 132
Majumdar, Prasanna, 128
Malkauns, 128–9
Mallick, Koel, 171
Mangeshkar, Lata, *86*, 194, *197*, 198, *199*
Mani, Karaikudi, *207*
Mansur, Mallikarjun, *124*
meditative surrender, 213
Megh, 131
Mehndi, Daler, *202*
Mishra, Nirmala, *127*
Misra, Sajan, *214*
Misrai, Hanuman Prasad, 25
Mission Ajoy, 36
Mitra, Dhirendra Chandra, *202*
Mitra, Suchitra, *202*, 203
Modi, Narendra, *203*
Moitra, Radhika Mohan, 53
Mother Teresa, *207*
Mukherjee, Adrija Nath, 51, 53
Mukherjee, Hemanta, 49
Mukherjee, Jatileshwar, 125
Mukherjee, Pranab, *203*
Mukherjee, Sandhya, 49, 205

Mukherjee, Sanjoy, *215*
Mukherjee, Shirshendu, *207*
Mukhopadhyay, Arati, *127*
Mukhopadhyay, Dwijen, *127*
Mukhopadhyay, Sandhya, *127*
Mukhopadhyaya, Manabendra, 49
Mulajore Kali Temple, *19*, 22, 33
Mumbai, 132, 187, 204
Music Today: Master's Choice, 138;
    Swar Utsav, 183
music, education for small children, 163;
    excellence in, 176; loving towns and cities, 120
Mymensingh, 15, 23, 52

N

Nachiketa, *211*, *127*
Nasreen, Taslima, *206*
Nat Bhairav, 53
national award, 128, 141–2
National Award for the Best Male
    Playback Singer, 128
nationalism, 15
Nazrul, 197
Nazrul Geeti, 131
New Orleans Jazz Preservation Hall, 195
Nishi Babu, *44*

O

omkar-based music therapy, 218
Onkarnathji, Sitaram, 78
Operation SandHI, 216–17

P

Padma Shri award, 194, *225*
Pal, Amar, *127*
Paluskar, D.V., *86*
Panigrahi, Raghunath, 49
Paramahansa, Ramakrishna, 22
Parekh, Asha, *209*
parents, 21, 24, 30–1, 37, 72, 76–7, 80, 88, 90, 94,
    99, 108, 138, 184–5
Parikh, Arvind, *211*
parivar parampara, 186
Patiala *gharana*, 122
Patiala Heritage Festival 2018, *138*
Patil, Pratibha, *194*
Patri, Satish Kumar, *210*
Peetham, Avadhoota Datta, *222*
Piya bholo abhimaan, 125
poetry, 212, 215
Poltu Da, 41

Pouchishe Baishakh, 51
Pradhan, Badal, *148*
Prasenjit, *171*
Premananda Tirthaswami Maharaj, as family guru,
    17–18, 21, 42, 116
prizes, 28, 30
public audience, 41

Q

Queen Elizabeth Hall, London, 131, 195

R

Raager Bahare, 125
Rabindra Bharati University in Calcutta,
    73, 76, 78, 97; MA in music, 76
Rabindra Sangeet, 58, 203
Rafi, Mohammad, 205
raga sangeet, 103, 111, 133, 197–8, 201,
    206, 208, 212, 216
ragas, 208, 213; archive for, 218; *Bhatiyar*, 38, 40,
    88, 90; *Bhoopali*, 38, 131; *dhrupad*, 22, 57,
    88; *Hamsanadam*, 182; *Jaunpuri*, 40, 89–90;
    Jhinjhoti, 205; *Khammaj*, 131, 203; *Malkauns*,
    205; *Maru Behag*, 183; *Yaman*, 40, 71, 203
Rageshri, 165
Rahman, A.R., *209*
Rajan, *214*
Ramprasad, Sadhak, 22
Ray, Bijoya, *133*, *201*, *219*
Ray, Satyajit, 128, *133*, 151, *201*, *219*
Ray, Sukumar, 28
record releases, 133
Rishith, 169
Riyaaz, 16, 70, 96, 100, 103, 146, 165, 201
Roy, Subinoy, 203
Royal Albert Hall, 195
Royal College of Music in London in 1990, 129
Rumi, Maulana Jalaluddin, 164

S

Sab sukh diyo kartar, 165
Sadananda Brahmachary Maharaj (*Guru*), *23*, *152*
Safar, 201
Saha, Samar 129
Saigal, Kundan Lal 21
Samanta, Pannalal (Pannu), 27–8, 32, 36, 42, 43,
    56; as formal guru, 27
Sangeet Natak Akademi Award, *183*
Sangeet Research Academy's Guru Ajoy
    Chakrabarty, 124
Sangeet Samrat Tansen, 189

Sanwariya anokhi tori chaturaayi, 128
Sargam, 25, 28, 150, 206
Sarkar, Jayanta, 128
Sarkar, Snehanshu Kumar, 155, 169
Sarnaik, Nivrutti Bua (Guru), *80*, 95, 152
Sealdah Station, 52, 83, 104
self-criticism, 115
Sen, Dilip, 195
Sen, Maya, 203
Sen, Mrinal, *206*
Sen, Niloy, 195
Sen, Shekhar, *211*
Sen, Shyamal K., *205*
Sen, Sumitra, 203
Sen, Surya, 16
Sengupta, Banasree, *127*
Shankar, Girija, (Guru) 49
Shankar, Ravi, 51, *86, 214*
Sharad Anjali, 125
Sharma, Shiv Kumar, 121, 193
Sharma, Sohan Lal, 89
Shrutinandan (A Musical Kingdom) 100, 123, 133,
    138, 142–4, 166, 170, 172, 175–6, 178, 181–2,
    184–5, 191–2, 198, 216, *218*; album launch
    of, *171*; Jnan Prakash Ghosh Sanctum, 166;
    memento of, *213*; studio, 193; system, 58,
    155, 169, 173; technique of, 173
Shyama Sangeet, 21, 131
Shyamnagar, 19, 22, 27, 33, 35, 37, 42, 48, 51,
    53–4, 61, 79, 94, 99, 103–4;
    Railway station at, 34
Singh, Jagjit, *210*
Singh, Manmohan, *203*
Singh, Ramdhari 'Dinkar', 107
Singh, Uttam, 198, *204*
singing, 213, 215; as 'on-air painting', 213
Sivamani, *204*
Sood, Daman, 187, 191, *211*
Sreemat Premananda Tirthaswamiji
    Maharaj, *18*
Stravinsky, 215
Subramaniam, L., *205*
sujanis, 23–4, 113
Sukumar's shop, 41
Sultana, Begum Parveen, 183
Suman, Kabir, *209*
Supriyo, Babul, *211*
Surer Surabhi, 125
swara, 25, 37, 43, 63, 69, 123, 125, 147, 172, 174,
    195, 201, 215, 220; patterns, 28, 70

T
table tennis, 73
Tagore, Abanindranath, 49, 51,
Tagore, Rabindranath, *51*, 164, 173, 176, 203–4;
    songs, 173, 197
Tagore-like moment, 83
tanpura, 30, 36, 74, 131, 148; from loan, 36
tappa, 57, 108
Tchaikovsky, 215
teaching music, 35, 38, 153, 155; as 'individual
    training', 170
Tejomayananda, Swami, 192
Thakur, Shrimati Tanima, 49–50
Theatre de la Ville in France, 195
Thirakua, Ahmedjaan, *86*
thumri, 57, 66, 108, 131, 133, 172, 183, 204, 218
Tollygunge, 99, 142; land offered at, 142
Tomari Gaahi Joy, 125
training, 40, 56, 71, 73, 88, 91, 94, 96, 169, 174
Tulsidas, 162
typing school, Shyamnagar, 79

U
Udhas, Pankaj, *207*
USA tours 131, *see also* Festival of India
Uthup, Usha, *205*
Uttar Pradesh Tourism concert by, 188

V
Van Beethoven, Ludwig, 133
Varma, Shrimati Manik, 49
Vatapi ganapatim bhajeham, 138
Venkataraman, R. *194*
Vijay, Kichlu (Guru), 88–91, 93–4, 103–4, 109, 117,
    121–3, 131, 151–2, 162–3, 166
Vivaldi, 215
Vivekananda, Swami, 22
vocal music, 50, 184, 215
voice, 21–2, 55, 60, 66, 71–2, 88, 96, 108, 114–15,
    170, 173–5, 188, 198
Vyas, C.R., 124

W
Wadekar, Suresh, *216*
western classical music, 215
Writers' Building, 16

Y
Yaad piya ki aaye, 131, 183